BETTER TOGETHER

BETTER TOGETHER

A Model University–Community Partnership for Urban Youth

Barbara C. Jentleson

Teachers College, Columbia University
New York and London

Published by Teachers College Press, 1234 Amsterdam Avenue, New York, NY
10027

Library of Congress Cataloging-in-Publication Data
Jentleson, Barbara C.
    Better together : a model university–community partnership for urban
youth / Barbara C. Jentleson.
        p. cm.
    Includes bibliographical references and index.
    ISBN 978-0-8077-5174-9 (pbk. : alk. paper)
    ISBN 978-0-8077-5175-6 (hardcover : alk. paper)
    1. Youth with social disabilities—Education (Higher)—United States. 2.
Urban youth—Education (Higher)—United States. 3. Educational equaliza-
tion—United States. I. Title.
    LC4091.J48 2011
    378.1'03—dc22   2010045270

ISBN 978-0-8077-5174-9 (paper)
ISBN 978-0-8077-5175-6 (hardcover)

Printed on acid-free paper
Manufactured in the United States of America

18 17 16 15 14 13 12 11   8 7 6 5 4 3 2 1

*To the Duke–Durham Neighborhood
Partnership, our community partners, and the
children of Durham*

Contents

Acknowledgments

The Duke–Durham Neighborhood Partnership was the work of talented, dedicated staff and community partners who created the afterschool and tutoring programs of Project HOPE. University and community partnerships depend upon administrative leadership for their survival and growth. The vision of Nannerl O. Keohane was instrumental in placing Duke–Durham community relations front and center as a priority of the university. In appointing John Burness to be the administrator for this effort, she found a tireless advocate for the partnership. John Burness championed the work of the DDNP and HOPE throughout the inevitable challenges faced by this university and community partnership. John worked to ensure that the DDNP and Project HOPE secured the administrative and financial support that was necessary for success and was the "fixer" of final resort to emerging problems. This necessary administrative leadership and support has continued under President Richard H. Brodhead, Provost Peter Lange, and Dr. Phail Wynn, Vice-President, Office of Durham and Regional Affairs. Our thanks to the W. K. Kellogg Foundation, Wachovia Foundation, and The Duke Endowment for their sustained funding support to the work of Project HOPE.

I could not have survived a week in the Durham community without the sure guidance given by Michael Palmer, Assistant Vice President and Director of Community Affairs. Durham is a community where every block and brick has a history, which makes it both a fascinating and perilous city to conduct community-based projects. Michael could always tell me the story and where I needed to watch my step. Sam Miglarese, Mayme Webb-Bledsoe, and David Stein are gifted community organizers, the best at what they do. Betsy Alden, David Malone, and Jan Riggsbee have supported the work of the DDNP and Project HOPE from its inception, lending their intellectual engagement, energy and commitment to all aspects of the work.

Project HOPE was fortunate in having a talented support staff who lived their commitment to the Durham community every day. Elizabeth

Henderson, Denice Johnson, and Helen Westmoreland worked with me to design and implement the infrastructure that made this complex project work so seamlessly. They loved being in the community working with our partners, afterschool students and Duke students. Their enthusiasm infused the work with the creativity, care and common sense that university and community partnerships need. Diann Walker and Betsy Wagner kept our fiscal management on track and within budget every step of the way.

The afterschool community coordinators were a professional and personal gift to the work of Project HOPE. Their dedication to the students and families is the foundation for all that is documented in this book. As other mothers of Duke tutors and the afterschool students, they provided daily life lessons in what it means to be a contributing member of a community that cares for its children. In addition, they met every documentation request, filled out all the forms and surveys, met with evaluators, participated in interviews, and wrote necessary reports and grants every year of the project. For myself, I simply loved every minute I got to spend in their relentlessly honest and caring company. Blessings and thanks to Betty Johnson (Crest St. Tutorial Project); Juanita McNeil (West End Community Center); Rebecca Oats, Wilhelmina Thornton, and Dosali Bandele (CommUNITY Scholars of Calvary Ministries); Gail Taylor (Carter Community School); Gwen Phillips and Donna Price (Northside Baptist Afterschool Program); and Marleah Rogers and Adam Eigenrauch (Emily Krzyzewski Center).

Marie Ellen Larcada, my editor at Teachers College Press provided support and guidance through each stage of writing the book. She is a gracious editor, who "got it" from the beginning and helped me craft a much better book. Thanks also to Nancy Power, Lyn Grossman, Shannon Waite, and Beverly Rivero for their assistance in producing the book.

Finally, my heartfelt thanks and love to my husband, Bruce, who has enthusiastically supported this project from the beginning. He knew that I was writing from the heart and provided necessary ballast through the moments of doubt involved in putting together a balanced presentation of this topic.

BETTER TOGETHER

Introduction

Duke University's freshman east campus is surrounded by a gray stone wall. For the past decade, during freshman orientation every August, Duke faculty and staff lead a group of about 100 Duke freshman through the gray wall into the Durham community. This group of students will go on to tutor for a semester in Durham's Public Schools and afterschool programs. They will experience firsthand cultural and learning differences, frustration, and the struggle to combine their youthful idealism with social realities. Their journey, and ours, begins when we take the walk beyond the wall.

The journey beyond the wall is the topic of this book. What is involved in leading students from the sheltered campus on one side of the wall into the diverse, challenging opportunities of the Durham community? How do university and community partners devise learning communities that are mutually beneficial for all participants? How does a university community build bridges from theory to practice, from knowledge to application, from knowing to doing?

The Duke–Durham Neighborhood Partnership (DDNP), initiated in 1996 under the leadership of President Nannerl O. Keohane, sought to engage community partners in the low-wealth minority neighborhoods immediately surrounding Duke University. Input from community partners resulted in identified areas of engagement addressing affordable housing, strengthening neighborhoods and health care access, and improved academic achievement of community youth. While developing the collaborative partnerships that addressed these significant issues, the university and the Durham community would also examine larger questions about the potential for mutually beneficial university and community partnerships.

This book presents a number of case studies encompassing the work of the DDNP and its involvement with the community-based afterschool programs sponsored by Project HOPE (Holistic Opportunities Plan for Enrichment). Project HOPE consists of six community-based afterschool programs designed to integrate community and university resources toward the purpose of improving the academic achievement of low-income minority youth. The afterschool programs were initiated by Durham nonprofit organizations with Duke University supplying tutors, operational funding, and program enrichment resources. This straightforward concept raised a host of complex issues about the nature of university and community collaborations that had no simple solutions. Like the Pied Piper in reverse, the children of Durham lured university and community partners into this project and have kept us grounded throughout its duration. Their youthful promise, energy, and enthusiasm challenged us to keep at it, plugging away at each of the project's challenges. Projects are successful because there is consensus around a common purpose, shared tasks, and ultimately, shared victories. We rejoice together now over each graduation, each good report card, and the health and growth of our children. Durham's children are the ultimate answer to each and every question and obstacle. We had to make this university–community partnership work because it matters. Afterschool programs became the vehicle, the interim space where the university and community could work out the answers to the tough questions of managing a university–community partnership.

My own involvement with Project HOPE began when the university received notification that the project had received significant funding from the W. K. Kellogg Foundation. As an educator for over 30 years, I entered the world of afterschool programming as an advocate with a healthy dose of skepticism. As an advocate, I was excited by the possibility of working with community partners who were willing to open their sites and provide a welcoming setting for students who could benefit from exposure to nurturing adults and activities. A more pragmatic view intruded as we surveyed our resources and could see all too clearly that project staff and community partners were trying to develop an infrastructure from a grab bag of tutoring, activities, and limited staff and volunteer resources. What I did not expect, but have immensely benefited from, was that I would learn what it meant to enter the community-based afterschool program setting, to work closely with community partners and their students, and to guide Duke undergraduate tutors as they worked with energy and capability to improve the outcomes for Durham's children. Along with the common tasks came daily surprises and inspiration and the creation of productive learning environments. In this learning process, we university and community partners asked ourselves and responded to many of the important questions facing collaborative partnerships and afterschool programs:

- What can afterschool programs do to promote positive youth development, particularly among low-income minority youth?
- What do community-based afterschool program settings offer that is unique?
- How do we successfully manage the complex collaboration and joint program administration that is necessary to sustain quality afterschool programming?
- Who learns? And what is learned? How do we develop communities of learning for all participants in the afterschool program setting?
- How do we create a culture of evaluation that supports program improvement and provides the information needed for external funding sources?
- What is necessary to sustain successful afterschool program networks, and how do we advocate for improved program quality? Can our programming be replicated in other communities?
- How does university–community engagement change the universities and communities, and what is the impact on student participants?

Although Project HOPE was primarily organized to deliver support services to Durham's community youth, it quickly became evident that this project would engage all participants in a steep learning curve. This was true for our university student tutors and project staff as well as the community-based staff and nonprofit organizations. The difficulties that arose and how they were overcome provide the basis for the practical lessons learned and the recommendations that are presented in each chapter.

The chapters are organized to describe the common issues and concerns of university–community partnerships and afterschool program development, as well as strategies for managing these issues and lessons learned through Project HOPE in the application of program practices. Each chapter weaves into its discussion the recommendations and best practices of the current research literature.

Chapter 1 discusses the history and current status of university and community partnerships. This chapter also provides case study detail about the scope of the DDNP and the context for Project HOPE.

Chapter 2 briefly examines the history and social roles of afterschool programs as they have developed over the past century. The pressing needs of out-of-school time and the potential of afterschool programs to address these needs are discussed as are the challenges facing afterschool programs today. This chapter also explores the thorny issues involved in joint program administration and collaborative university and community partnerships. Afterschool programs often exist in uneasy collaborative partnerships with other community organizations and social institutions. In this chapter is a frank discussion of common program administration problems and tension points, and strategies for addressing these problems in order to build sustainable beneficial program practices. Although the case study focus is afterschool programs, the lessons learned are applicable to many issues in collaborative university–community partnerships.

Chapter 3 examines the university and community engagement dynamic, and describes the extensive learning communities that evolved as a result of this interactive engagement. Service learning and civic engagement were a particular focus of Project HOPE that, from the beginning, presented both challenges and remarkable opportunities for growth to all involved partners. All participants were learners over the course of this project, sometimes painfully so, and this chapter discusses the role of service learning and civic engagement within university and community partnerships.

Chapter 4 describes the construction of an ongoing, formative evaluation process in community-based settings. The research, development, and necessary adjustments involved in gathering qualitative and quantitative data in the fluid, dynamic community-based afterschool program setting is explored in this chapter. The university and community partners worked together to untangle a series of knotty evaluation difficulties and came to develop the skills, formats, and collection strategies necessary to build a sturdy evaluation foundation that informs internal program improvement and external funding sources.

Chapter 5 is an overview of the major challenges and opportunities facing university and community partnerships and their challenges in promoting the successful development of quality afterschool programs in our communities today. This overview examines the extensive work of the DDNP at the end of its first decade and its strategic planning for the next decade. The narratives, data, and voices shared throughout this book were gathered with the intention of expanding the dialogue between universities and their communities. The experiences of the DDNP have resulted in multiple reciprocal benefits for Durham and for Duke University, and in exploring that story we hope to provide insights into what has been learned and what still needs to be done to improve ourselves and the lives of others.

CHAPTER 1

How Do We Become Better Together?

The growing movement from isolated, insulated ivory towers towards societally-connected, socially-responsible higher eds engaged in school-community-university partnerships is largely a response to the marked disjunction between the promise and power and the actual performance of American higher education, particularly its research universities.
—Ira Harkavy, "School-Community-University Partnerships"

Everyone in Durham has a Duke story. Sometimes it's a positive story and sometimes it's a negative one.
—Michael Palmer, Director of Office of Community Affairs

The case for building robust and positive university–community partnerships is grounded in the urgency of current social realities. For an increasing number of American universities, particularly those located in major urban areas, this reality has been that of declining economic conditions in their host communities. As major social institutions, which cannot readily move, university campuses must deal with the issues of the decaying physical environments, growing poverty and crime rates, and the failing public schools of their surrounding neighborhoods and communities. Public scrutiny can also be a force that exposes the jarring inequities of wealthy private universities with their rich human, intellectual, and technical resources existing alongside some of the nation's poorest communities. Universities also carry the additional responsibility for working closely with the next generation of our country's professional leadership during their formative years. Civic and social responsibilities combined with enlightened self-interest is forging a renewed interest and investment in university and community partnerships (Bok, 1990; Harkavy, 1998).

HISTORIC ROOTS OF
UNIVERSITY–COMMUNITY PARTNERSHIPS

The role of universities in society has historically reflected the needs of our rapidly emerging and changing society. College and university development in the colonial period was focused on the training of ministers and civic leaders. This was followed in the 19th century by a concern for educated citizens who could fill the growing community needs for teachers, doctors, ministers, engineers, and lawyers. In our nation-building phase, American society was focused on the practical needs of the nation and universities were charged with the mission of serving our developing society (Harkavy, 1998, Spring, 2005).

Daniel Coit Gilman, the founding president of Johns Hopkins University, stated in his inaugural address the broad hope that "universities should make for less misery among the poor, less ignorance in the schools, less bigotry in the temple, less fraud in business, and less folly in politics" (Boyer, 1994). In the late 19th and early 20th centuries, the major urban universities—Johns Hopkins, Columbia, the University of Chicago, and the University of Pennsylvania—viewed their primary purpose to be the advancement of knowledge that would improve the quality of life in American cities. The city itself was viewed as an ideal site for putting knowledge into action. The possibilities for integrating theory and practice were a driving force in this progressive vision of the university's role in society.

World War I brought this applied view of the university's role and responsibilities to a weary end. Complex social problems proved to be a surprisingly difficult laboratory, with the move from theory to practice being a good deal messier in a community setting than in a university classroom or laboratory. University research in the midcentury moved to experimental approaches that could be more precise and verifiable. The increased focus on the pursuit of pure knowledge over applied knowledge came to be firmly embedded in the rewards and advancement processes of the university, which in the long term has led to less direct involvement and responsiveness to addressing societal needs (Bok, 1990; Boyer, 1994; Harkavy, 1998).

University involvement in research that focused on society's issues often followed funding source directions. The organization and funding of scientific research by the National Science Foundation, U. S. Defense Department, National Institutes of Health, and Centers for Disease Control are prominent examples of these trends. Government funding has been more sporadic and difficult to sustain in the social sciences. The War on Poverty and Project Headstart are examples of initiatives whose funding has significantly fluctuated (Bok, 1990). Foundation funding in the social sciences has also faced significant limitations. Foundation priorities shift, with resources following the most recent set of priorities. Foundation funding cycles tend to be short term, with 1- to 3-year cycles being the norm. This leaves limited time for programs addressing complex issues to grow, learn from their mistakes, and develop mature structures capable of longer term sustainability (Bok, 1990, Fleishman, 2007).

By the latter half of the 20th century, social problems began pressing against the gates, walls, and ivory towers of major research universities. Poverty, racial inequality, distressed neighborhoods, and public education issues were clearly demanding engagement, forcing universities, once more, to turn at least part of their attention to the host communities whose taxpayers support them.

Bok (1990) makes the observation that American universities enroll over 12 million students with over 700,000 faculty. He asks us to consider whether all of these faculty need to be focused on pure research and scholarship. Couldn't some of their intellectual, financial, and technical resources be returned to the communities and taxpayers who support them? Strand, Marullo, Cutforth, Stoeker, and Donohue (2003) state that, at this point, few faculty have the training or experience to conduct field-based coursework or research. How can they be expected to move into this new area or to train their students to be effective practitioners without significant incentive structures to take on these new and very necessary tasks?

Since 1989, universities have begun to respond to these challenges and to address the question of how they can become better together with their communities. Benson, Harkavy, and Puckett state that "universities constitute such remarkably fragmented, self-contradictory, internally competitive and conflicting institutions that they tend to move with all the speed of a runaway glacier" (2007, p. 79). Even so, the question was being asked on campuses of how universities, communities, and civically engaged citizens can become better together. Maurasse (2001) did a comparative study of four representative universities and their attempts to construct positive university and community partnerships. The University of Pennsylvania, San Francisco State University, Xavier University, and Hostos Community College each developed different strategies to improve their host communities while sustaining their primary educational mission as universities. These partnerships addressed a wide range of community issues including affordable housing, health care, public education improvement, neighborhood revitalization, and economic development. Rodin (2007) provides invaluable detail in her book about the University of Pennsylvania's community engagement during her presidential tenure. The remarkable revitalization of West Philadelphia and the University City neighborhoods is a welcome example of the mutual benefits that can exist when universities become significantly engaged with and respond to community problems. It will become necessary for a national dialogue to develop that examines the common themes, solutions, and adaptations that universities and communities must make if they are to continue working together. Faculty who are involved in community-based projects and research can be critical sources of knowledge and technical skills regarding what works and what doesn't when developing programs and projects to resolve community issues. There will also be an increased need for sustained funding to support university and community engagement. Consistent, long-term support of program initiatives are critical to the success of partnerships and the institutionalization of university–community partnerships (Maurasse, 2001). Duke University has been an active participant in the effort by major research universities to develop productive, positive university–community engagement, and their efforts have their own fascinating integration with Durham's history.

DEVELOPMENT OF THE
DUKE–DURHAM NEIGHBORHOOD PARTNERSHIP

During the 1980s and 1990s, Duke University began to examine and mend its relationships with the Durham community. Like many other universities, Duke's host community of Durham was undergoing a period of economic and social transition. These changes forced its community and university leadership to undertake an often painful and painstaking examination of their relationship and to work together carefully toward a more constructive and healthier collaborative partnership. This challenging and rewarding journey has been grounded in the individual relationships and arrangements constructed through the Duke–Durham Neighborhood Partnership (DDNP).

"I don't know anything about Durham, and I don't know anything about the Civil War," was the exasperated comment of a Duke student who was diligently attempting to design lesson plans in a DDNP summer camp. Why did a teacher of young children in a summer camp environment need to know Durham's social history to function effectively? What did she need to *know* in order to *do*?

Understanding Durham's rich social history requires at least a rudimentary knowledge of the Civil War, of the role of tobacco and textile factories in southern industrial development, and of civil rights history. Current community dynamics contain critical elements of this history and have been documented in multiple books and documentaries about Durham. Washington Duke, the founder of Duke University, made his fortune in the tobacco and textile industries in the early 20th century. Along with his sons, James B. Duke and Benjamin N. Duke, the Duke family was responsible for the rapid development of the Durham community and two universities, Duke University and North Carolina Central University. The Duke family was convinced of the importance of education in improving the economic and social conditions in the South. In the Indenture establishing the Duke Endowment, James B. Duke (1987) remarked: "Education, when conducted along sane and practical, as opposed to dogmatic and theoretical lines is, next to religion, the greatest civilizing influence" (p. 233). In accordance with this pragmatic vision, he commented that:

> The courses at this institution be arranged, first, with special reference to the training of preachers, teachers, lawyers and physicians, because these are most in the public eye, and by precept and example can do the most to uplift mankind, and second to instruction in chemistry, economics and history, especially the lives of the great of (the) earth, because I believe that such subjects will most help to develop our resources, increase our wisdom and promote human happiness. (p. 233)

The first trustees of the Duke Endowment added to these practical sentiments that the development of the university would be directed "with a view to serving conditions as they actually exist" and would be "for the use of all people of the State and Section without regard to creed, class or party, and for those elsewhere who may seek to avail themselves of the opportunities it has to offer" (Durden, p. 133).

Economic development continued apace with Duke University's development for much of the 20th century. The tobacco factories and related industries in Durham provided employment for both white and black workers, and this led to the growth of a significant black community in Durham. This bustling community gave rise to a prominent, prosperous African American community. Durham was an active participant in the major civil rights battles of the 1960s and remains a community that, as stated by a Duke student observer, "faces its problems and tries to do something about [them]." Although Durham is a midsized city of around 200,000, the university and its medical centers are the largest employer in Durham and the second largest employer in North Carolina.

By the 1980s, Duke University was faced with the glaring discrepancy of a major research university located in an ethnically and socioeconomically diverse community with a host of problematic social issues. These included closed textile and tobacco factories, economic and health care inequities, poverty and racial inequalities, deteriorating neighborhoods, rising crime rates, and failing public schools. Durham is also located at the nexus of two major interstates, I-40, (east–west) and I-85 (north–south), making it a logical distribution center for drug trafficking between Washington and Atlanta. Finally, there was limited access to corporate partners. Although Research Triangle Park is home to prominent national and international corporations, these are often branch offices whose resources and community involvement are usually shared between the three cities (Raleigh, Durham, and Chapel Hill) that make up the Triangle.

While Durham's economic and social trajectory was reflecting a downward trend, Duke University's trajectory was definitely on an upward trend. When Nannerl Keohane became Duke's president in 1993, the trend lines were defined by Durham's decline and Duke University's rise to national prominence. Within the Durham community, Duke's reputation as an exclusive campus was reinforced physically by the gray stone wall surrounding its east campus and the heavily wooded areas enclosing its west campus. President Keohane made the decision to make the improvement of relations with the Durham community a priority of her presidency. Moving from good intentions to an engaged community partnership would raise a host of questions for Duke University administrators, trustees, and community partners. A major goal in the earliest and most difficult days of the partnership was enlightened self-interest and the increased public scrutiny brought on by Duke's national prominence. Three core questions needed to be addressed at this early juncture:

1. What would it take for the lead administrators of a private university to be significantly engaged with the Durham community?
2. How does a university community, with its wealth of knowledge, skills, and resources, learn to put aside its mantle of "expertness" long enough to listen to community partners with their own

wealth of knowledge and experience on what it needs to be a better place to live, raise families, and educate its young people?
3. What and where are the places where engaged partners can meet
and work on common problems and solutions?

An answer to the first question is that it takes the leadership of the
university stating publicly that improved university and community relationships are a priority. President Keohane (2006) took this significant
step in her inaugural address:

> We must recognize the impact of what we do here on our neighbors and
> on the quality of the society in which we live. Members of our univer-
> sity and community are engaged in many forms of civic service, drawing
> skills and energies directly from their work as faculty members, students,
> and staff. Our Medical Center provides care and healing every day for
> many people who cannot afford to pay.
>   Universities cannot single-handedly solve all the problems of our so-
> ciety. Our resources are limited and they are mostly given to us for other
> purposes. But we depend heavily on the quality of life in our region, and
> in partnership with government, business leaders, and interested citizens,
> we can work to develop coordinated programs for addressing some of the
> most urgent problems in education, housing, violent crime, health care, and
> other areas of direct concern in the city of Durham, our home. (p. 224)

The second important step was for the leadership to initiate a planning
process and action plan that would provide the necessary support and
resources to sustain the stated priority over an extended period of time.
President Keohane worked with the university's Board of Trustees to
fulfill these requirements, and, in December 1994, a long-range plan was
approved by the board. Among its six priorities was included a focus on
improving the university's engagement with Durham:

> Particularly in its most local surroundings, the university must strive con-
> stantly to play a constructive role as a good citizen of the Durham com-
> munity. While we must be concerned about the quality of life in all of
> Durham, we must be particularly concerned about the quality of life of our
> employees and of the neighborhoods immediately adjacent to our campus.
> (Burness, 1996)

According to President Keohane, what was needed next was a framework
that would structure Duke University's engagement with Durham. John
Burness, Duke's Senior Vice President for Public Affairs and Government
Relations, was assigned the task of putting together a working team and

strategic plan for community engagement. In February 1996, he was responsible for the appointment of the Community Relations Planning Committee. The CCR Committee had the benefit of input from two leading elected officials who were no longer in office, William (Bill) Bell, a 22-year veteran of the Durham County Commissioners, and Sandy V. Ogburn, an 8-year veteran of the Durham City Council. Burness (1996) noted that Bill Bell and Sandy Ogburn were both community activists with long histories of working with the community. They had the necessary credibility to work with community members and university staff "to create a process of long-range planning of Duke–Durham community relations and to present its best thinking on what plan we should pursue to focus and improve the positive impact Duke has among its neighbors" (interview, July 21, 2009).

Over a 2-year period, Bell and Ogburn completed a report on their meetings and discussions with community members in 12 neighborhoods near the Duke campus. The report included a matrix of each neighborhood's stated issues and concerns. This matrix would become the framework for the work of Duke University's Office of Community Affairs and the DDNP.

WHO WERE THE NEIGHBORS?

The neighbors of the DDNP were geographically defined as those communities that immediately surrounded Duke University's east and west campus (see Figure 1.1). Similar to the University of Pennsylvania's strategy, Duke University made the decision to focus on these neighborhoods in order to maximize the impact of the DDNP activities. John Burness stated that the challenge and scope of the problems in these communities was best approached by concentrating on the neighborhoods adjacent to campus, where the university could develop the necessary relationships and apply the appropriate strategies to begin to make a difference for community members. Lessons learned could then be translated into models and practical solutions that could be expanded into Durham and the region. Michael Palmer, the director of the Office of Community Affairs, defined this strategy as the "touches" that were needed to build relationships and trust with community members. According to Palmer, the role of the DDNP was to increase the number and positive quality of direct human touches with community members that would add to and gradually improve the Duke–Durham story.

FIGURE 1.1. Duke–Durham Neighborhood Partnership Map

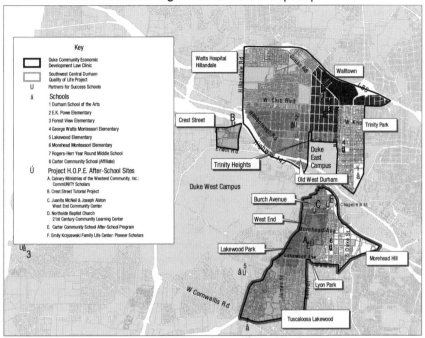

With regard to the second question—How can a university learn to put aside its mantle of "expertness" so that it is able to respectfully develop responses to stated community needs?—John Burness stated that the first step of the Community Relations Committee was to let the neighborhoods tell their Duke stories—to let all the history, much of it bad, come out, and to listen carefully to neighborhood concerns before rushing to craft solutions. Comments from community members that are noted in the Community Relations Committee matrix and meeting minutes give a sense of the historic depth of the distrust and negative impressions of Duke University.

Mary Duke Biddle Trent Semans consented to be interviewed for this book and was gracious with her time as always. Mrs. Semans is the matriarch of the Duke family, and she lived and raised her family in Durham. She has long been active in Durham affairs and served on the City Council in 1951. In recalling the period before the DDNP, she related an incident during the early 1990s that brought the history of university and community relations home for her. While attending a community event, she was confronted by a community resident with the blunt question, "What do we do together?" She responded with examples that she could quickly recall involving medical care and the arts, but knew these were bright spots that were few and far between. The resident responded, "Glad you pointed that out, but there should be more." Mrs. Semans agreed, but noted that Duke's efforts were too isolated to have an impact. She stated, "There was nothing you could touch." Not all encounters were as polite as this one. John Burness commented that a good sense of humor and the hide of an elephant were important when working through the earliest Duke–Durham conversations. Residents' comments were included in an appendix to the Committee for Community Relations planning document (Burness, 1996).

> There is a general mistrust of Duke's intention. *All said* (author's italics) that past history has been one of poor communication, [with] no follow-up communication, [and that it was] difficult to know who to speak with at Duke.
> There is a great deal of suspicion about Duke based on past history. . . . There was frustration expressed that there was no "one stop shopping" at Duke and it was difficult to *know* who one needed to talk to for any particular issue/item.
> There is a great deal of suspicion of Duke by this neighborhood. People in Walltown do not feel what they do as a neighborhood is respected by Duke—their contribution is not valued.
> Concern that in the past Duke has not communicated effectively about what is happening on campus that affects neighborhoods outside the campus.
> The longstanding issue is that of student parties which frequently last until 5:00 A.M. and the attendant problems of noise, trash, abusive language, greater levels of debauchery than in past years, [particularly] excessive drinking [and] underage drinking.
> Skeptical that Duke is undertaking this effort in an attempt to takeover their neighborhood for more campus space.

A common theme running through the community's stated concerns is raised in question 3: Who does one talk to at Duke, and how does one meet with them? There had to be a designated office staffed by individuals who could develop and maintain credibility with community residents as the sustained work on community problems was developed. The answer to question 3 regarding what and where this work would happen would become the work of Duke's Office of Community Affairs and the DDNP. It was crucial in these early days to design a "bottom up" strategy, where the ideas and resources of the university could be matched with community priorities. Each of the DDNP neighborhoods has a story and will be briefly described to give a sense for the complexity of the issues facing the DDNP.

Crest Street

The Crest Street neighborhood has a distinctive tradition of self-reliance and speaking truth to power that has led to its current stability of a predominantly owner-occupied neighborhood. The Crest Street Neighborhood Council is a strong community organization that continues to support its maintenance as a cohesive community. Crest Street began as a small African American neighborhood within Durham's white mill community in West Durham. When the planned construction of the Durham freeway from 1960 to 1970 threatened to eliminate the Crest Street neighborhood, the residents banded together and hired a young lawyer, Mike Calhoun, who used civil rights legal provisions to block the building of the highway. Duke University took the position of opposing the freeway completion, but worked to develop solutions to the legal impasse. The solution that emerged was to move existing housing and develop new housing on an alternate site behind the Duke Medical Center. Mr. Willie Patterson, president of the Crest Street Neighborhood Council, worked to develop a respectful working relationship with the university that has resulted in mutually beneficial programs and activities for the Crest Street neighborhood. The stated issues of this community were

- technology resources and training;
- tutors and mentors for community youth;
- access to Duke athletic camps;
- health clinic for neighborhood elderly and poor.

Northwest Central Durham (Walltown, Trinity Park, Trinity Heights, Old West Durham, and Watts/Hillandale)

This neighborhood has a mixture of housing that changes in character from block to block. In 1998, the traditionally black Walltown neighborhood had 79% of its population with incomes below the poverty line. Its ties to Duke University go back to its founder, George Wall, the talented carpenter who helped build Duke University and whose family was the early backbone of the Walltown neighborhood. Bounded on three sides by more prosperous white neighborhoods and Duke University's east campus, Walltown residents have a deep residue of suspicion of the university's intentions and are concerned that the university will overwhelm the neighborhood.

The Trinity Heights and Trinity Park neighborhoods were established by professional, prosperous, predominantly white families who built the large, solid homes that dominate these neighborhoods. In 1910, the construction of a new campus of the Watts Hospital, which is now the North Carolina School of Science and Math, gave rise to the Watts/Hillandale neighborhood. The development of the Hillandale Country Club and golf course confirmed the predominantly white, middle-class status of this neighborhood.

The issues confronted by this neighborhood were marked by distrust over Duke's role as a landlord and by often contentious interactions with rowdy Duke students. Early in its history as Trinity College, Duke bought property adjacent to the campus. When land prices skyrocketed, Duke bought other land south of Main Street and built its current west campus. The former property, bordering Walltown, was left undeveloped and neglected over the intervening decades. Neighborhood issues for these residents would be persistent and thorny. For Walltown, there was suspicion that Duke would eventually expand its campus and overwhelm the Walltown neighborhood. In the 1970s, there was a study by consultants that called for Duke to acquire the land around the east campus and near the city for future expansion. It was never adopted, but it was known to exist, and it raised suspicions about Duke's plans. The poverty of this neighborhood resulted in problems with affordable housing, crime, and education, which were overwhelming to intermittent volunteer efforts.

The issues of concern to Walltown residents were

- access to medical care;
- affordable housing; and
- tutoring and mentoring of neighborhood youth.

The issues of concern to Trinity Heights and Trinity Park residents were:

- crime;
- raucous student parties;
- rental housing being taken over by student housing; and
- parking and speeding on cross streets.

Southwest Central Durham (Burch Avenue, West End, Lyon Park, Lakewood, & Morehead Hills)

Southwest Central Durham is another mixed income housing area of Durham. Similar to other geographic areas of Durham, the area developed along racially divided lines. The predominantly black Burch Avenue, West End, and Lyon Park neighborhoods represented the lower end of the socioeconomic spectrum, where the reported 1990 median income was $14,180 and unemployment was double the area rate. Over 60% of this area was renter-occupied, which contributed to the need for considerable rehabilitation of older housing stock.

Other neighborhoods of Southwest Central Durham were comprised of some of the oldest and most fashionable neighborhoods in Durham. Forest Hills and Morehead Avenue contained the homes of former wealthy Durham residents such as Benjamin N. Duke and William T. Blackwell. A large amusement center, Lakewood Park, was located at the trolley terminus, which provided easy access to Durham's downtown and work areas. The large black population of this area worked in the homes, businesses, and factories of Durham and had no access to the amusement park. Durham residents today tell of growing up next to the large and attractive amusement park but being unable to participate in its delights. This was a glaring example of the rigid segregation that existed during this period. Another significant community landmark in this neighborhood was the Lyon Park Elementary School, the traditional elementary school that educated generations of Durham's black residents. The neighboring recreation area had been maintained by neighborhood volunteers, but, with desegregation, the school was mothballed and fell into disrepair. The neighborhood defined its issues as

- lack of constructive activities for neighborhood youth;
- rehabilitation of the Lyon Park Elementary School;
- day programs for the elderly;
- too much rental property leading to instability; and
- laundry trucks traveling through the Burch Avenue neighborhood.

The Neighborhood Meeting Report matrix, which recorded these issues in a condensed format, would become the guiding framework for the DDNP. Initially, Sandy Ogburn was hired to continue as the first head of the newly formed Office of Community Affairs. In 1999, after Sandy Ogburn resigned in order to focus on other community work, Michael Palmer was hired out of Durham county government to be the next director of the Office of Community Affairs. Palmer states that his work in local government and stint as interim County Manager had given him the opportunity to observe what government could do to respond to community needs. He became interested through his work on county projects in DDNP neighborhoods in improving and increasing the impact of university resources on community problems. With initial decisions made to create the Office of Community Affairs and to define the work of the DDNP to confined geographic boundaries, the DDNP then devised guiding principles for its work with community partners.

So, with map and matrix in hand, the DDNP needed to decide how to go about conducting collaborative partnerships with community residents and organizations. The DDNP was cognizant of the view commonly held in the Durham community of Duke University as "the plantation." The cultural baggage and power imbalances implicated by this perception led the DDNP to set initial rules of engagement with community partners that would build mutual respect and trust over the long term. Provost Peter Lange, in his reflections about this period, stated that "it was important to strike the right balance between two themes: self-interest and public service." He further commented on the importance of John Burness's absolute insistence that the DDNP agenda be taken from the community. DDNP operationalized its activities with basic guidelines that provided structure for community partner and university staff interactions:

- listening to community partners and being responsive to their stated needs;
- supporting projects that were developed with partners in response to their stated needs;
- continuing emphasis on process over product, which might slow initial project implementation but would lead to longer term sustained success;
- emphasizing community control over projects, with the university as a background partner;
- limiting direct partnerships to only those neighborhoods in the immediate Duke University vicinity to enhance impact.

The earliest and most prominent efforts of the DDNP were focused on affordable housing and redevelopment in DDNP neighborhoods. An early and enduring partnership with Martin Eakes, founder of Self-Help Corporation, led to the development of long-vacant land in Walltown into faculty and staff housing in Trinity Heights. Further initial financing led to the brokering of former rental housing to low-cost affordable housing for Duke University employees and community residents. These efforts have grown exponentially in Walltown and expanded to the West

End community and neighborhoods. Collaboration with the Self-Help Corporation, the Durham Land Trust, and Habitat for Humanity expanded the availability of affordable housing in these DDNP neighborhoods. A recent 10-year evaluation indicated that over 264 affordable housing units had been built or rehabilitated and were accompanied by rising property values and lower overall crime rates in these neighborhoods. These early successful initiatives gave the DDNP the momentum it needed to address another priority, closing the achievement gap for minority youth in Durham.

The State of Durham's Children 2000 Report compiled significant statistics that emphasized the need for community attention to its youth. Among the report's findings were a low unemployment rate (2.1%) but one of the highest child poverty rates in North Carolina at 19.1%. High rates of school suspensions (12.1%) were reported for middle and high school students, with 70% of those suspended being African American males. Although difficult to report accurately, unacceptably high dropout rates that were 27% higher than the state average were noted. African American students were dropping out at a rate that was three times higher than that of their white counterparts (Reiter-Lavery, Rabiner, & Dodge, 2000). In response to these and other data, Ann Denlinger, the superintendent of Durham Public Schools, announced the goal in 2002 of ending the minority/white achievement gap by 2007. Each of these factors created significant momentum toward developing school-based tutoring programs and community-based afterschool programs that would support positive youth development in Durham. Recruiting, training, and supervising tutors and mentors would raise a host of infrastructure, program administration, and funding issues for the DDNP.

An important aspect of the developing DDNP story is that, in the initial planning years of the Office of Community Affairs, there is scant mention of the DDNP's work and its relation to the academic mission of the university. In President Keohane's inaugural address and in some of the meeting comments, there is recognition of the individual efforts of faculty, staff, and students with the Durham community. These efforts were often too scattered or intermittent to create the sustained partnerships needed to address complex community needs. Although the university was clearly working hard to listen and respond to emerging community partners, the concept that the university could engage with the community in ways that would enhance university student learning and civic engagement was not an initial priority. One source of this early caution was related to the community's perception that prior research

had been "done to" community members and that they resented being
treated like "lab rats." An initial task of the DDNP's engagement with
the community would need to be respectfully conducted with "touches"
that established trust and relationships. Several of the communities
noted that the students in their communities needed tutors and mentors. Three communities—Crest Street, Walltown, and West End—had
already started afterschool programs hoping to address the academic
needs of their students. West End had noted to the Community Relations
Planning Committee that "they appreciated the student volunteers from
Duke, but thought they needed better training."

Duke's development office had targeted the W. K. Kellogg
Foundation as a possible source for funding that would address the
educational needs of DDNP students. Mimi O'Brien headed the development office's work with the community and she formed an advisory
committee to begin conceptualizing a grant proposal that would lead
to reflective community-based educational programming. Synergy was
beginning to form around the development of this grant that would
enhance the emerging service learning and civic engagement movement
at Duke University. Duke had a thriving Community Service Center
under the capable leadership of Elaine Madison that organized student
and staff volunteer efforts in the community. Rev. Betsy Alden, hired in
1997 as the university's director of the Office of Service Learning, was
operating under the aegis of Dr. Elisabeth Kiss, the newly appointed
director of the Kenan Institute of Ethics. Their collective aim was to
"infuse the curriculum with ethical discourse." Rev. Alden came to
Duke University as a third-generation Duke alumnae who had a national reputation for developing extensive service-learning programs
in the community college system. Her wide-ranging experience with
service learning in an academic setting made her an effective advocate
for integrating service and civic engagement into undergraduate coursework. Dr. David Malone, director of Duke's Program in Education, was
the faculty sponsor for Partners for Success, a tutoring program where
students taking education courses were required to tutor in Durham
Public Schools. These advocates would be responsible for initiating the
internal dialogue integrating service to community with the academic
coursework and undergraduate life of the university. The support of
lead administrators—Dr. Willam Chafe, vice provost for Undergraduate
Education and dean of Arts and Sciences, and Robert Thompson, dean
of Trinity College—provided early encouragement and resources for
service learning and its role in undergraduate education.

John Burness, Peter Lange, and Mimi O'Brien (from Duke's development office) planned a trip in the winter of 2001 to the W. K. Kellogg Foundation in Battle Creek, MI. According to Lange, it was a cold trip balanced by the warm reception from the Kellogg Foundation staff. His goal was to pitch the work of the DDNP, which he states was easy because he was enthusiastic and in agreement with DDNP goals. The two major goals stated in the grant proposal were (a) to develop community-based educational programming that would support the improved academic achievement of Durham's low-income minority youth, and (b) to engage the talents and skills of the university's undergraduate students, under faculty supervision, with community-based afterschool programs.

Funding was granted and scheduled to begin in the fall of 2002. The plan became known as Project HOPE (Holistic Opportunities Plan for Enrichment), and its two major goals would form the cornerstone of the project, with additional components woven into this fundamental programming. Duke's Community and Family Medicine Department, under Susan Yaggy, would develop the health components of HOPE programming. This would include the opening of two school-based and two community-based health clinics. The clinics would be open to all Durham students and community residents, regardless of income. Further social services would be provided by the Center for Child and Family Mental Health, a consortium funded by Duke University, the University of North Carolina–Chapel Hill, and North Carolina Central University.

The Kellogg Foundation linked funding to Duke University and North Carolina Central University, forming a joint effort to improve the academic achievement of Durham youth and to investigate methods for increasing university and community engagement. Throughout the duration of the project, these two universities collaborated in their programming efforts, and they continue to do so. The stated goals of Duke University's Project HOPE were to

- promote the academic achievement of Durham children and youth living in the DDNP area;
- increase university and community engagement;
- encourage changes in institutional policies; and
- explore lessons learned about university and community engagement.

Project HOPE was designed to create an engagement infrastructure that would be sturdy enough to sustain community youth through the developmental tasks of childhood and adolescence. Duke University was viewed by community partners and community leaders as a major resource for the Durham community. It was vitally important that the nature and process of university–community partnerships be carefully and reflectively implemented. With these aims in mind, the work of Project HOPE began in the fall of 2002. University gateways began to creak open, with community and university gatekeepers keeping a watchful eye on the unfolding process.

CHAPTER 2

Whose Program Is It Anyway?

For adolescents growing up in poor urban communities, the youth center as home-place also provides a valuable bridge to the outside world. One of the hardest tasks for social policy has been to find ways in which young people can feel connected to the wider society. Social scientists have referred to this feeling as a sense of social integration. Community-based afterschool programs can serve as a setting in which youth connect with broader social institutions and the wider adult community.

—Barton J. Hirsch, *A Place to Call Home*

AFTERSCHOOL PROGRAMS AS COLLABORATIVE PARTNERS

Project HOPE focused its energies on the development of community-based afterschool programs as a direct response to the stated needs of its community partners. These community organizations stated clearly that they wanted to help the students in their community succeed academically and socially, but that they wanted to provide that support in their community settings. Several of the organizations already had afterschool programs but needed additional resources and tutoring assistance for their students. Their strong preference for community-based afterschool programs coincided with emerging research supporting the role of afterschool programs in supporting positive youth development. Afterschool programs can provide a useful community-based social structure that can significantly support low-income children and their families (Chung & Hillsman, 2005; Fashola, 2002; Vandell & Shumow, 1999). Afterschool programs can support positive youth development by providing academic tutoring and social skills mentoring that promotes good work habits, positive peer and adult relations, and exposure to cultural enrichment activities. Maintaining relationships with afterschool program staff can assist children and youth in their negotiating the social institutions of the wider

community. Older youth can be assisted in developing job skills, finding employment, and guidance in developing post secondary career plans
(Cooper, Valentine, Lindsay, and Nye, 1999; Forum for Youth Investment,
2002; Halpern, 1999; Hirsch, 2005).

Numerous challenges arise, however, in creating and sustaining
quality afterschool programs that will achieve the academic and social objectives desired by many communities. Some of these challenges
are improving the quality of afterschool programs; obtaining sustained
funding and resources; recruiting and retaining trained, dedicated staff;
evaluating programs for program improvement; and reporting to external funding sources. These challenges can be overwhelming to community-based organizations (CBOs), which often lack the infrastructure
and resources to sustain quality afterschool programs.

As community leaders, policymakers, and community members examine the current role of afterschool programs in their respective cities
and towns, it will be an important reminder that this is not a new social
phenomenon, but rather a durable social institution that has provided
crucial safety and learning environments for America's youth through
a significant portion of our history (Bodilly & Beckett, 2005; Halpern,
2003). In virtually every American community there exists a range of
afterschool programs, all of which share common components (Hirsch,
2005; Noam & Tillinger, 2004):

- flexible infrastructure, which is able to be culturally responsive to
  local community needs;
- appealing activities that can attract and retain community youth;
- activities that can be complementary and supportive of school
  system objectives.

There is growing evidence that afterschool programs are of special
importance to today's minority youth, providing a "second home" or
"intermediary space" that can be critical for their development. Noam,
Miller, and Barry (2002) state that:

> There is some evidence that afterschool programs can provide a much-
> needed link between values, attitudes, and norms of students cultural com-
> munity and those of the culture of power. (The culture of power refers to
> belief and expectations transmitted by dominant social groups; p. 14).

Current Social Realities Affecting Afterschool Program Development

Changing social forces of the 1960s–1970s significantly altered the
American family structure as increasing numbers of American women

were drawn into the labor force. By 1997, 78% of married mothers with school-age children were working outside the home (Capella & Larner, 1999; Vandell & Shumow, 1999). Remarkably, the major social institution providing supervision of school-age children, the American public school, has operationally remained unaltered in the same time period. The school day is shorter than the typical office work day, and the academic school calendar remains a 10-month schedule, leaving a summer gap of almost 2 months in most communities. Recent research demonstrates that there is academic loss during the summer months, negatively affecting both math and reading achievement for American students. Middle-income students are better able to sustain reading levels over the summer months, while low-income youth suffer academic loss in both reading and math achievement, exacerbating a persistent achievement gap. (Cooper, 2001a).

American families struggle to piece together a patchwork of child self-care, activities, and partial supervisory arrangements to cover the gaps left by school and work schedules. This social shift has resulted in the afterschool hours of 3–6 P.M. emerging as a particularly vulnerable time period for community youth. In this time period, juvenile crime rates spike dramatically as documented by the juvenile justice system nationally. The nature of the crimes happening during the afterschool hours are serious and violent in nature, including murders, rapes, robberies, and aggravated assault. America's schoolchildren, left without adult supervision during the afterschool hours, are most likely to

- become victims of violent crime;
- be in or cause a serious car accident;
- be killed in a household or other accident; and
- experiment with dangerous drugs.

An emerging research consensus (Chung & Hillsman, 2005; Newman, Fox, Flynn, & Christenson, 2000) indicates that afterschool programs can respond to this social need and have been able to

- reduce juvenile crime and violence;
- reduce drug use and addiction;
- reduce other risky behaviors (smoking and alcohol abuse); and
- boost school success and high school graduation

A second emerging pattern is that middle- and upper-income families seem to be putting together a workable patchwork of afterschool care, lessons, and extracurricular activities that minimizes the need for daily structured afterschool programs. Students in middle- and upper-income families have the means to pay for lessons or buy uniforms or other equipment necessary for participation in extracurricular activities, and have better access to transportation to and from activities. Often these families live in communities and neighborhoods where there is quality afterschool programming and recreational facilities.

A third pattern is that low-income children who are shown most able to benefit from afterschool programs often have the least access to this valuable resource. Recreational resources are often fewer and less appealing in lower-income neighborhoods. For many children, the program fees or equipment needs are beyond their means. Transportation access may also be an issue, and parents may feel that it is not safe to allow their children to walk or travel to and from the recreation programs that do exist. Finally, lower income children may be needed at home to take care of younger children or to assist with home chores (Bouffard, et al., 2006; Halpern, 1999; Mahoney, Eccles, & Larson, 2004).

Low-income families are significantly disadvantaged by the current social constructs. Parents, whether married or single, may be working more than one job to remain economically afloat. Often the work is shift-based or otherwise inflexible. This reality combined with traditional school operating hours creates a situation where many low-income children are spending significant time in self-care or fluctuating supervisory arrangements. The best available national surveys on the regular use of self-care by school-age children (ages 5–14) indicate a prevalence of at least 12% (3.7 million in 1995). Some incidence of self-care by preschoolers (1%) is a source of significant concern. More than five times as many children of single, employed mothers are left alone after school (Kerrebrock & Lewitt, 1999; Vandivere, Tout, Capizzano, & Zaslow, 2003).

Of critical importance is the afterschool program's ability to serve as an intermediary social setting where low-income students and families are physically, psychologically, and culturally comfortable. A second benefit is that structured afterschool programs are able to support the school's academic mission by providing academic support and an intermediary role between the school and community youth. When problems arise, afterschool programs can provide the intermediary space needed where sensitive issues can be addressed and resolved (Hirsch, 2005; Noam, Miller, & Barry, 2002).

In addition to inflexible operating hours, the current school trend emphasizing standardized curriculum with test score results dominates many aspects of school functioning and has created increased pressure for children to perform academically as measured by standardized testing measures. The school day is increasingly devoted to the improvement of test scores, with less time spent on academic areas or enrichment activities that are not measured by tests. Afterschool programs can be partners to school systems by providing tutoring and academic support during nonschool hours and by supplementing social skills development. This has come to be defined by the Harvard Family Research Project as a "complementary" learning function. Complementary learning "acknowledges significant contributions not just of schools, but also of families, afterschool programs, and other community supports for increasing children's success in learning and in life" (Kakli, Krieder, Little, Buck, & Coffey, 2006).

Afterschool programs are uniquely placed in our society to work as productive engagement zones, particularly to vulnerable low-income community youth. Afterschool program structure is less defined and more fluid in nature, so interactions are more informal and boundaries are blurred and more unstructured (Pittman, Irby, Yahatem, & Wilson-Ahlstron, 2004). Resource and funding constraints, while a primary difficulty for most afterschool programs, also create a force for openness, experimentation, and creativity. An informal mindset develops that creates greater tolerance for unconventional ideas and activity combinations (Halpern, 2003; Noam, Miller, & Barry, 2002).

Community-Based Afterschool Programs as Cultural Brokers

Community-based afterschool programs are commonly autonomous nonprofit organizations that become resource and cultural gatekeepers to their afterschool program site. CBOs are independent organizations that function as cultural brokers in their respective communities (Cooper, Denner, & Lopez, 1999). Their gatekeeper role introduces an important element of cultural asymmetry where outside groups wanting to work at afterschool program sites have to ask permission to gain access to youth participants and programming. In CBO spaces, cultural dominance shifts with community youth and their families becoming the dominant, representative culture, and outside partners or agencies becoming "guest partners." This cultural shift is particularly important when the outside partner is a traditionally dominant one, such as a university, government agency, or private foundation.

In the cultural broker role, a host/guest formality can be introduced to the partnership. Issues of respect and trust exist, so that formal courtesy is initially evident and permission must be given to get to a state of more relaxed informality. Other trust issues such as showing up daily and doing the necessary work, also lead to building productive relationships on shared projects. As Noam and Tillinger (2004, p. 87) state, "Development of trust needs to be nurtured, requires time and personnel required to build relationships." The shared daily work of program administration creates an atmosphere of common, equal enterprise. Through working together to manage children, implement activities, and share in communal celebrations, partners also promote shared feelings of joint accomplishment. Both within the community and with external partners, CBO staff become viewed as community assets and leaders. Afterschool site coordinators are positive role models able to teach survival and negotiating skills to youth as they address the developmental tasks of childhood and adolescence (Anderson, 1999; Hirsch, 2005).

Community-based afterschool programs are an effective, intermediary space for concerned community members to develop and implement programs that benefit community youth. A shared interest in youth welfare naturally creates communication that bridges diverse cultures, professional training, and power balance discrepancies. Emergent common ground can be developed around the focused areas promoting youth development. The Project HOPE model experience that is discussed in the following chapters describes how several community-based afterschool programs evolved to create and expand a collaborative and growing common ground for diverse community partner organizations focused on the common goal of supporting community youth.

Increasing Parent Involvement in Education

Community-based afterschool programs are also engagement zones that provide critical support to low-income families. Community-based afterschool programs can be contact zones for their respective communities where there is shared language, social interactions, and similar religious and cultural values. The programs are typically managed and staffed by members of the community who are proven, trusted leaders. Family members view the staff as social models and will seek assistance from them in dealing with problems of raising children and youth (Cooper, Denner, & Lopez, 1999; Tucker & Herman, 2002).

Low-income families can receive support directly through services and activities offered in community-based afterschool programs. Working families may not have the funds or time to provide lessons, transportation, and support for their children to be involved in extracurricular activities and skills development. Family members working more than one job or caring for ill family members may find it difficult to take their children to museums or to participate in area cultural events. Family members may not possess the educational experience, time, or energy to help their children with homework or to fill out the necessary applications and other procedures for admittance to special schools or academic programs. Commenting on trips that she has taken with her afterschool students and their families, one of HOPE's coordinators commented, "I'm educating the parents as well as the children." In discussions with the parents, she noted that many of them did not take trips because of the lack of time and resources to organize this type of travel.

As accepted and trusted partners, community-based afterschool programs are well-positioned to use valuable afterschool and summer vacation time to supplement school and family efforts to promote positive learning opportunities for community youth. Through tutoring and academic assistance, community-based afterschool programs can help students consistently and accurately complete their homework and build their literacy and math skills. In addition, they can work directly with parents and school personnel to monitor and assist students through academic difficulties.

Through improved family engagement practices, afterschool programs can assist family members in their efforts to promote academic and social success for their children. Because afterschool programs can organize activities during nonschool and nonworking day hours, these are potentially more flexible programming hours for community youth and their families. The activities can be less formal and have a broader definition. Engaging families may involve

- providing more opportunities for families to spend time with their children (e.g., cookouts; joint visits to museums, parks, or recreation play facilities such as bowling alleys or skating rinks);
- learning about children's schooling by accompanying parents to school conferences and holding parent information sessions periodically;
- receiving support for life needs such as connecting families to local food banks, social services, and medical services;
- seeking parent participation in decision-making through periodic surveys, parent meetings, support groups, and parent-organized events (Kakli et al., 2006).

Community-based afterschool programs provide a valuable infrastructure for communities to use as sources of support and engagement networks for youth. They are a dynamic engagement zone that, at their best, can promote collaboration from multiple sources in support of positive youth development. Community-based afterschool programs are organic to their respective communities and have locally based organizational support. While the structure is often loose and informal, there is usually enough structure that programs and participants can be sustained. Communities often have enough space in their community centers, churches, and schools (when not in session) for creativity and age differentiation in program development. Because the CBO is supported by its own community, there is often enough drive to promote program growth and learning. Through its children, the community's future is at stake, which creates a powerful incentive to sustain the afterschool programs.

CONSTRUCTING A COLLABORATIVE FRAMEWORK FOR AFTERSCHOOL PROGRAMS

Afterschool programs frequently exist within uneasy collaborative partnerships. With limited funding and resources, they are forced to partner with other institutions, agencies, or organizations in order to survive. The continuous search for sustainable resources places them in a vulnerable and often defensive posture where they are in competition with other programs seeking funding from the same sources. This is not an atmosphere that lends itself to the trust and relationship building that is necessary for collaborative partnerships to succeed.

Noam and Tillinger (2004) detail these and other difficulties in their article defining a theory and typology of collaborative partnerships in afterschool settings. They note that afterschool program partnerships have been little studied until recently, and that the current business and social service delivery literature on collaborative partnerships is difficult to apply in the afterschool program setting. Afterschool programs frequently lack the staff to create and sustain partnerships and may also be hampered by minimal supportive organizational infrastructure. In spite of the difficulties in managing collaborative partnerships, afterschool programs have much to gain from the cooperative effort involved in a partnership. There is potential for a decreased sense of isolation, increased resources, and the power of joint community advocacy to improve afterschool programming.

Universities are uniquely positioned within many communities to provide expertise, resources, and funding that are valuable to CBOs. They are beginning to grapple with the opportunities and challenges of addressing the needs of the community where their institutions reside. University and community partnerships encounter specific structural and cultural difficulties that need to be recognized and addressed throughout community-based collaborative partnerships. Basic questions arise that need to be answered effectively if campus and community partnerships are to be sustained and productive:

- What are the basic guidelines for conducting collaborative campus and community partnerships?
- How do these principles translate into an operational framework that involves program administrative tasks, legal agreements, and resource management?
- How are the staff and volunteers (campus and community) to be organized? And who is responsible for their supervision and support?

Strand et al. (2003) discuss the basic principles of community-based research and how collaborative campus and community partnerships can provide unique opportunities for reciprocal learning. These authors provide basic guidelines for the development of collaborative partnerships covering the areas of entering partnerships, conducting partnerships, and what the outcomes of such partnerships can accomplish. The guidelines provide a useful framework for discussing university–community partnerships and are presented in Figure 2.1.

FIGURE 2.1. Project HOPE Partnership Model

Entering Partnerships	*Conducting Partnerships*	*Outcomes of Partnerships*
• Share a worldview	• Share power	• Satisfy each other's interests and needs
• Agree about goals and strategies	• Communicate clearly and listen carefully	• Have their organizational capacities enhanced
• Have mutual trust and respect	• Understand and empathize with each other	• Adopt a long-range social change perspective
	• Remain flexible	

Source: Strand et al., 2003.

Entering Partnerships—What Can We Do Better Together?

Strand et al. (2003) stress the importance of initiating university partnerships with discussions that determine a shared worldview between university partners and CBOs. This involves agreement on the nature of the problem and similar views on the solutions. From these beginning discussions, the university and community partners can then begin to develop goals and strategies for solving the identified problem. All parties involved need to be committed to the devised work plan and willing to commit their time, talent, and resources to the work of the partnership. This is a leap of faith for all partners. Regardless of past experiences, at this point, there is a need for enough mutual trust and respect to move into the initial commitments of the project. From its inception, Project HOPE fit Weiss's (2005) description of a "community of practice":

> Communities of practice are groups of people who share a concern, set of problems, or passion about a topic and who deepen their knowledge and expertise in this area by interacting on an ongoing basis. Communities of practice are composed of members with diverse backgrounds and perspectives. These members find common ground in their commitment to an issue and work together to build a knowledge base that can inform their collective interests and individual work. They do this through sharing experiences and information, exploring common challenges, giving advice and suggesting strategies, generating new ideas and engaging in collective practice. Successful communities of practice rely on dialogue and genuine relationships. Members are connected not just by formal commitments but also by the value they place on learning together.

Some of Project HOPE's community partners had small afterschool programs, while other community organizations expressed the desire to start afterschool programs. Both types of community partners needed additional resources and consulting support. It's important to note here that Project HOPE grant funding and the university academic year began in August 2002. In its first year, university project staff and community partners decided to begin placing Duke student tutors in afterschool programs even though HOPE's basic administrative framework was not in place. The reason for this decision was that the HOPE project administrator felt that community partners needed to see service delivery action upfront in order to establish a pattern from the beginning that service to Durham students was the primary focus of the project. Duke

University's Program in Education had a successful tutoring program in Durham Public Schools called Partners for Success, developed by Dr. David Malone, the director of Undergraduate Studies for Duke's Program in Education. This model consisted of Duke undergraduates taking education courses that had a service-learning component requiring students to tutor and mentor 3rd–5th graders in Durham Public Schools geographically located in the DDNP. The student tutors received course credit for their tutoring hours, but no payment. Project HOPE began its first year using the Partners for Success tutoring model to develop tutoring programs that would work in the afterschool programs of DDNP community partners. This initial effort was very limited in scope, involving one education course each semester (with approximately 25 students) and three community-based afterschool programs with 102 youth participants. Additional university and community resources were provided to the afterschool programs but on a very limited, incidental basis. This strategy worked. By providing service delivery first, with flexible follow-up planning for program improvement and evaluation, the first step was taken in establishing that Durham students were the primary focus of the collaboration.

At the same time, Project HOPE began to develop a formative evaluation process that would provide continuous evaluations to community partners, Duke faculty and staff, and outside funding sources. The evaluation had the following components:

- ongoing reflective process activities that would inform internal and external practice;
- data collection and documentation that would be the basis of both internal and external reporting of student and program processes;
- documentation as a source for continual improvement strategies— program improvement as a formative process;
- Reporting to existing funding sources and as a foundation for seeking additional funding sources.

From the outset HOPE staff needed to deal with the community partner perception that evaluation was a burdensome, intrusive process and that they objected to being treated like "lab rats." The partners could recount numerous negative experiences with university researchers where this had been the case. Restoring the evaluation dynamic to a productive process that developed positive results for student participants and continuous program improvement was a major accomplishment of the university–community partnership. This process and its products are discussed further in Chapter 4.

Conducting Partnerships—Who Is Really in Charge of the Program?

Strand et al. (2003) discuss the importance of conducting partnerships in a manner that will lead to sustained commitments between university and community partners. This is an example of beginning with the end in mind. Community partners with prior experience with university researchers are highly aware of grant funding cycles and university research priorities that may not be effective in addressing community needs. Community partners wanted to know if Project HOPE was going to be a partner for the long haul *and* if it shared their commitment to the daily, often tedious work of program administration. This required establishing administrative procedures and processes that could be sustained over years of collaborative partnership.

As was also discussed by Strand et al. (2003), community partners needed concrete evidence throughout the project that university partners would share control in project operations. Operationally, this required trusting and respecting the experiential knowledge that community partners have of their neighborhood, organizations, and local agencies and institutions. Communication required discussions without jargon, clearly stating issues and problems in a manner that invited feedback. Listening carefully and responding with understanding and empathy also required taking time to find out what was really going on in the lives of community partners and their organizations. Flexibility in program design and execution was evidence to community partners that project staff understood and were responsive to their needs. Communication, sharing control, developing mutual understanding, and demonstrating flexibility were critical to launching and sustaining Project HOPE.

Program administration required working across cultural boundaries on a regular basis. The university and community partner demographics were dramatically different, with the afterschool program staff being predominantly African American women and the university project staff being predominantly Caucasian women. This shifted over time, with the afterschool program staff and university staff developing some ethnic and gender diversity. Ethnic and cultural differences made initial contact and communication somewhat reserved, but respectful. As the project got underway, common ground and productive communication patterns were established that promoted freer and more open exchanges of ideas and feedback. These exchanges could prove startling and often required a sense of humor. An example of one common tension that existed was over HOPE's insistence that Duke students tutor one student per tutoring session. Community coordinators would sometime ask tutors to allow other students to join in these tutoring sessions. When this didn't work out particularly well, the Duke students would usually air their concerns with their faculty mentor. Conversation follow-up with the afterschool site coordinator would result in comments like, "Why didn't the student come to me first?" or "What's wrong with the tutors that they can only teach once child at a time?" Frank discussions of the limitations and expectations of the tutors would follow and program changes were made as necessary. Over time, all involved got better at judging tutor capacities and making placement adjustments during the semester.

Project HOPE's structure initially evolved out of the grant administration requirement that Duke University be the grant administrator and manager of financial resources and reporting. This dynamic was balanced by having the CBOs function as the afterschool program administrators and granting them autonomous authority in the management of their programs. From this starting point, a negotiated administrative structure emerged with defined roles and responsibilities for university and CBO staff. School system responsibilities were limited initially to providing information on student progress and behavioral issues. As the afterschool programs became effective, school system personnel became more responsive to afterschool program and university staff. The Project HOPE collaborative staffing model (Figure 2.2) evolved quickly over the first 2 years and was firmly established by the third year. This negotiated administrative model has sustained the collaborative partnership for over 7 years, demonstrating a flexible structure with clearly defined roles and responsibilities for university and community partners. The remaining chapter narrative describes these roles and responsibilities in more detail as well as the significant tension points that needed resolution to ensure the partnership's success.

CBO roles and responsibilities. The CBO's primary responsibilities covered the management and control of the afterschool program facilities and its daily operations. Each CBO hired and supervised its afterschool program staff, which consisted of professional and paraprofessional members of the CBO's community. Each CBO developed

FIGURE 2.2. Project HOPE Collaborative Staffing Model

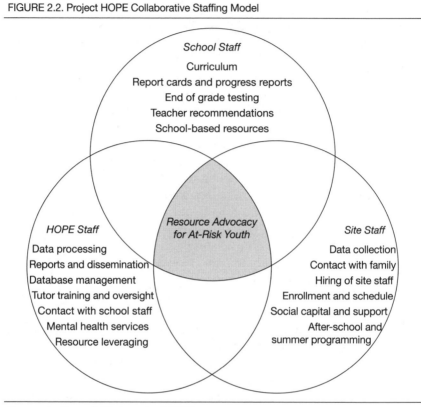

School Staff

Curriculum
Report cards and progress reports
End of grade testing
Teacher recommendations
School-based resources

HOPE Staff

Data processing
Reports and dissemination
Database management
Tutor training and oversight
Contact with school staff
Mental health services
Resource leveraging

*Resource Advocacy
for At-Risk Youth*

Site Staff

Data collection
Contact with family
Hiring of site staff
Enrollment and schedule
Social capital and support
After-school and
summer programming

Source: Jentleson & Westmoreland, 2005.

additional volunteer staff from their communities who could be called upon to help when necessary. The CBOs were also responsible for the on-site, daily supervision of university tutors with the assistance of HOPE staff and faculty.

CBOs were responsible for the planning and implementation of a daily schedule and activity flow. Some consultation with HOPE staff was involved in order to create a smooth flow with the tutoring program, and this required some adjustments to match undergraduate student class schedules. Although the majority of HOPE programs are conducted from 3 P.M. to 6 P.M., they are not all operational Monday–Friday. Also, one HOPE program is conducted in the evening from 6:30 to 7:30 and on Saturday mornings, from 10 A.M. to noon. Final decisions about operating hours and program activities resided with the CBOs' program coordinators.

CBOs were also responsible for the organization and use of instructional materials, reference materials, and computer and software operations. Project HOPE staff consulted and advised the CBOs' staff in these areas and assisted in the purchase of the academic materials. The CBOs acted as gatekeepers for all resource activities conducted in their programs. Typically, HOPE staff would inform coordinators of an available resource, and the coordinator would decide if it was a resource they could use. Once the decision was made to accept the resource activity, HOPE staff would facilitate the initiation of the activity in the afterschool program, and the site coordinators would manage the implementation of the activity. The CBOs and project staff would exchange feedback on the resource activity, with recommendations on whether it would be useful for other programs. A similar process was followed for outside agencies and other collaborative activity participation. This has been one of the most successful aspects of the university–community engagement process, with the university acting as the gateway to the program partners and the CBOs acting as the gatekeeper for their specific programs. The process has resulted in a dramatic and sustained increase in resource activities being conducted in DDNP afterschool programs (see Table 2.1 later in this chapter).

Finally, the host CBO was responsible for the internal fiscal management of the afterschool program. CBOs were also responsible for all aspects of reporting to their respective boards or other agencies. Typically, the evaluation and fiscal reporting requirements for Project HOPE grants administration were used to fulfill internal reporting and fiscal requirements as well, leading to greater efficiency in program documentation efforts and improved capacity building infrastructure of the CBOs.

University roles and responsibilities. The primary responsibilities for the Project HOPE faculty and staff involved grant administration oversight, fiscal management and distribution, tutor program management, and collaboration with school system personnel. The initial W. K. Kellogg grant was supplemented in successive years by additional private foundation funding and government funding from the Wachovia Foundation, the Duke Endowment, and the 21st Century Learning Centers. As these diverse funding streams developed, financial management and grants reporting became a significant responsibility for HOPE and DDNP staff.

During Year 1, the Office of Community Affairs staff worked closely with Duke University's law clinic to develop Memorandum of Agreements for community partners and Outside Service Agreements for outside contractors. These became the primary oversight documents for the project. The Memorandum of Agreements and the Outside Service Agreements were renewed annually, giving both partners the opportunity to continue the working arrangement and to make adjustments as necessary. Initially, this seemed to be a legalistic and cumbersome formality. However, in time, these agreements became a basis for establishing a professional working partnership that was more objective and ultimately respectful of each organization's responsibility. The Community Affairs staff implemented financial distribution to the CBOs, and financial audit oversight was conducted by the financial departments of Duke University and/or the funding source accountants.

It should be noted here that the After School Corporation, a much larger afterschool program network located in New York City and New York State, reports a similar structure in its management of multiple funding streams and resources with over 100 program sites and CBOs. The burden of seeking financial resources, navigating financial and legal requirements, and administering multiple grants is a task that can be overwhelming to nonprofit CBOs, which are primarily focused on program service delivery. A significant lesson learned was that universities have professionally trained accounting, legal, and development staff who can be directly involved in this aspect of project management as a portion of their overall responsibilities. Both a large flagship program such as the After School Corporation and a smaller fleet program such as Project HOPE found this to be operationally efficient and, ultimately, a way of sustaining and increasing a range of resources to afterschool program partners (Friedman & Bleiberg, 2002).

Tutoring program management quickly evolved into a primary responsibility of Project HOPE's university staff. The initial pilot period of placing Duke undergraduate tutors in the community-based afterschool programs was successful and logistically manageable. The HOPE site coordinators enjoyed working with the tutors and the tutors enjoyed working in the afterschool programs with the youth participants. The more informal afterschool program setting presented challenges, but the opportunity for providing significant academic support and the freedom to be innovative proved to be an excellent opportunity for community and university partners.

School system roles and responsibilities. Afterschool programs benefit from strong collaborative partnerships with school system personnel. However, both school-based and community-based afterschool programs struggled with program administrative and communication issues. Afterschool program staff needed to have curricular alignment, updated homework information, report card grades, and test scores in order to effectively serve their program participants. Getting this information to flow smoothly and consistently throughout the school year was a significant challenge for afterschool program staff. For example, the six Project HOPE afterschool programs served as many as 37 public, charter, and private schools in the Durham area. The logistics of contacting each school, let alone each classroom teacher, were not manageable for afterschool program staff. By the second year, the university project staff was able to designate a single staff member as the school liaison coordinator, whose primary job responsibility was school system contact and database management. This innovation made it possible to develop effective administrative and communication networks.

The school liaison coordinator was crucial to building a bridge between the afterschool coordinators and school system staff. The school liaison coordinator developed a one-page Individual Student Plan that contained vital information about each student's academic progress. This included report card grades, end-of-grade test scores, and teacher comments and recommendations for student work. Getting this basic information after the first reporting period in the fall provided the school liaison coordinator with the data needed to concentrate on students who were struggling. Site coordinators and tutors were able to continue working with students who were making good academic progress, while the school liaison coordinator followed up with the teachers who were reporting student difficulties. This set up another responsive loop, with teachers able to see follow-up and results from their communication with the school liaison coordinator. Afterschool coordinators received the information they needed to support their students. Parents were also able to have more informed conversations with afterschool and school personnel regarding their student's school progress.

Once this looping was established, teachers communicated much more freely with afterschool personnel and university project staff. Their enthusiasm helped the school liaison coordinator in her work with school office and administration in acquiring test scores or additional school information and resources. As usual in these circumstances, a moment arrives when project staff know that the collaboration is working well. For the school liaison coordinator, this happened during the start of a recent school year, when a teacher chased her down the hall to let her know about a student she was recommending for the program. It should be noted that the school liaison coordinator was an unfailingly gracious individual who was respectful of staff needs and time constraints. This included small incentives (a ream of copy paper, colorful sticky notes, a raffle for handmade jewelry, etc.) that give the process a personal touch and let teachers know their hard work and cooperation was appreciated.

By Year 2, the tutoring program in HOPE became a launching point for a range of university and community engagement activities. With the HOPE infrastructure beginning to take shape, it was possible to actively recruit and promote tutoring activities within the university context. The Program in Education quickly integrated further service-learning components into a broader range of its course offerings. These tutors and activities were generally offered either in Durham Public Schools classrooms or HOPE afterschool program sites and were supported by HOPE and the Program in Education staff.

Communication facilitates collaborative partnerships. Ongoing communication, both informal and formal, is the foundation of every aspect of productive university/community engagement. The communication needs to be direct, open, and responsive. The talk needs to be followed by actions that produce desired results or a clear explanation of what is happening to prevent the desired outcome. HOPE staff attempted to keep communication channels flowing consistently, with the understanding that no communication network is perfect.

Formal communication involved Memoranda of Agreements, regular fiscal invoicing, and monthly evaluation reporting. Group coordinator meetings were held monthly. These were luncheon meetings with a formal agenda that included a monthly site update by each coordinator, which involved discussions of current or emerging site issues, titled by the group as "the good, the bad, and the ugly." HOPE staff used some of the meeting time to present opportunities or resources that had become available to the afterschool program. Finally, the external evaluator scheduled regular site observations and interviews with each program site coordinator. These results were shared regularly in formal written reports.

Informal communication occurred as the HOPE staff conducted weekly site monitoring visits. Project HOPE staff met internally every week and held a weekly discussion covering the sites that had been visited and which ones needed to be seen. Trouble-shooting occurred during these discussions and covered a wide range of problem areas—no problem was off limits. It was at this time that decisions were made about who was going to address what problem and whether other community affairs personnel were needed to help solve the existing problem. During the weekly site visits, coordinators often brought up issues to discuss with HOPE staff. Prompt attention to the details of program management addressed the bulk of short-term issues. Persistent or longer term issues usually become the provenance of the larger community affairs staff. This is because the larger issues (e.g., physical space, funding resources, computer labs) required broader community intervention than could be managed by the HOPE staff. The supportive role of the broader community affairs staff was critical to the project's success. This staff included colleagues who also were active in the Durham community and who were working on community activist issues such as better housing and health care, neighborhood improvement, cultural enrichment, school system and technology advancement, CBO capacity-building, and fund-raising. These activities operated as a supportive infrastructure to virtually all aspects of Project HOPE.

Outcomes of University and Community Partnerships—Who Benefits?

In discussing final principles, Strand et al. (2003) state that in order for partnerships to be sustained, they need to be mutually beneficial. Campus-community partnerships are sustainable when there are benefits to all partners that are worth the time, energy, and funding that it takes to sustain the collaboration. For university partners this involves improved student and faculty learning, faculty publications, improved civic engagement for students and faculty, and an improved campus image in the community. Community partner organizations can benefit from improved service delivery, access to greater resources, enhanced organization capacity, and strong advocacy for community problems.

Project HOPE experienced these expected benefits and an overall positive synergy that was the foundation for new projects and initiatives throughout the university and community. Resource development and management became a significant component of Project HOPE administration. While it is challenging to track all the ways that resources

TABLE 2.1. Project HOPE Resources Chart, 2002–2007

Duke University Departments	*Resources Provided*	*02-03*	*03-04*	*04-05*	*05-06*	*06-07*
Athletic Department **D**	Tickets to football and women's basketball games				X	X
Education	Student tutors; faculty consultations	X	X	X	X	X
Child and Family Health	Social skills classes; individual assessments		X	X	X	X
Community and Family Medicine	Neighborhood clinics; health education classes		X	X	X	X
Community Service Center	America Reads/America Counts Tutors	X	X	X	X	X
Center for Child and Family Policy	NC Data Research Center		X	X		
Center for Documentary Studies	Visual and media projects		X	X		
Drama Department	Theatre classes	X	X	X		
Duke Performances	Tickets to performances; artists classes		X	X	X	
Facilities Management	Property improvement and landscaping	X	X	X	X	
Fraternities	Recreational activities for students		X	X	X	
Hart Leadership	Coordinates research service-learning projects	X	X	X	X	X
Institutional Equity	Diversity training; EDI Award			X	X	X
Kenan Institute for Ethics	Coordinates research service-learning projects	X	X	X	X	X
Law Clinic	Memorandum of Understanding with partners	X	X	X	X	X
Instructional Technology	Donated and repaired computers	X	X	X	X	X
Duke Medical School	BOOST (math & science education); dental hygiene			X	X	X
Romance Languages	Student tutors from Spanish classes			X	X	X
Student Affairs	Community service projects	X	X	X	X	X

Duke Student Partners	*Resources Provided*	*02-03*	*03-04*	*04-05*	*05-06*	*06-07*
Black Student Alliance	Holiday arts and crafts; talent show				X	
CLICK	Computer literacy classes		X	X		
Club Tennis	Tennis lessons	X	X	X	X	X
Durham Giving Project	Duke student fundraising for community activities		X	X	X	X
Girl's Club	Middle school mentoring activities		X	X	X	X
Law Students	MLK Day Fair				X	X
Multicultural Dance Club	Dance activities				X	X
Project CHILD	Freshman volunteer student tutors	X	X	X	X	X
Robertson Scholars	Organize activities with Carter Community School			X	X	
Student U	Summer school organized by Duke students					X
Swim with the Blue Devils	Swim lessons with Duke diving team				X	X
University Scholars	Tutoring services	X	X	X		
WOODS	Outdoor recreation activities	X	X	X	X	X
Woodsmont	Outdoor recreation fair on Duke's campus	X	X	X	X	X

Durham Community Support	*Resources Provided*	*02-03*	*03-04*	*04-05*	*05-06*	*06-07*
Carolina Circuit Writers	Artist-in-residence programs					X
Carolina Theatre	Performance tickets					X
Dept. of Public Health	Pregnancy prevention program	X	X	X	X	X
Dept of Social Services	Referral source for social worker			X	X	X
Durham Arts Council	Artist-in-residence programs			X	X	X
Durham Police Department	Crime prevention demonstration	X	X	X	X	X
Durham Public Schools	Teachers consultation on student progress	X	X	X	X	X
Emily K. Foundation	Afterschool program development			X	X	X
Fusion, Inc.	Translation and cultural programming		X	X	X	X
Hispanic Education Initiative	HEI Resources Fair			X	X	X
Legacy Foundation	West End Center renovation				X	
Museum of Life and Science	Museum tickets			X	X	X
NC Cooperative Extension	Teen retreat; camp challenge; ASAP				X	X
NC Central University	Saturday academy; 21st century centers, early college	X	X	X	X	X
UNC–Chapel Hill	Student volunteers; grant preparation			X	X	X
Walltown Children's Theatre	Dance, piano, and drama classes	X	X	X	X	X

have been drawn into Project HOPE, Table 2.1 shows a chart tracking resources that are directly involved in service delivery in the six Project HOPE sites. The degree to which these resources, once initiated, have sustained their involvement with the afterschool programs is a testament to the role of a supportive community–campus administrative infrastructure that sustains program involvement.

The role of program documentation and evaluation is a major component of HOPE program management and is discussed in greater detail in Chapter 4. The HOPE external evaluators held a mirror up to our programming efforts at consistent intervals from the beginning. By consenting to be participant observers, they were integrated into the continuous communication and feedback loop that was an enormous benefit to all program participants. Although they worked informally with us throughout the program year, they submitted formal reports midyear and at the end of the academic year. Their observations and findings were openly shared and discussed with the community partners, HOPE and community affairs staff, the DDNP Advisory Board, and funding agencies.

TENSION POINTS

Cross-Cultural Contexts

There were numerous cultural differences between the university and the CBOs that needed to be recognized and worked with throughout the university and community engagement process. The importance of establishing mutual respect, trust, being active in relationships, and staying the course were important for developing the common ground that is the foundation of university and community engagement. For the purposes of this project, prior negatives had to be overcome, as the community partners each had negative experiences that inhibited their initial interactions. This was where empathetic listening and responsive programming were important. However, it needs to be noted that Durham community partners were a seasoned group of community activists. Although listening was important, timely service delivery, financial support, and responsive problem-solving were the ultimate keys to success.

Attention to cultural differences became a focus of Duke undergraduate coursework. It quickly became evident that Duke students often had limited experience with tutoring and mentoring minority students and scant direct experience in community settings. Through training, coursework, readings, and discussions, students and community partners were provided the opportunity to express their observations and concerns. The result was to bring into the open fascinating topics and issues for all participants. Sample student reflections demonstrate the type of cross-cultural issues that emerged during tutoring experiences in the after-school programs:

> *We have difficulty dealing with the great diversity in our country.* Issues such as the cost of helping English language learners and special needs children are not ones we can simply throw money at to cure; there is a lot of work that will have to be done to improve the education of these groups of learners.

> *How do different learning styles and environments directly affect students?* We focused on numbers, trends, and statistics in class, but going to the center and seeing personally how children were affected made the problems more intimate.

> *The role of adults in the continuing education of children.* We really do have to try and make this a better place for our kids, and that starts by teaching the younger generation how to flourish in our world.

An early emphasis on direct service delivery (tutoring, instructional materials, funding, and staff devoted to the project's administration) with follow-up evaluation procedures made it clear that HOPE placed the needs of Durham youth as its major priority. This is consistent with a formative evaluation approach that emphasizes internal program improvement and is more consistent with community-based research project goals. The community-based research model quickly established the common ground of collaboration and action toward improving the lives and outcomes of our children and youth.

School System Interactions—Who Are You and Why Should We Pay Attention to You?

A significant point of tension that frequently emerged in the after-school program collaboration was interaction with the public school system. Both public schools and afterschool programs are often underresourced and overcommitted, with too few staff to perform their responsibilities well. While this is not exactly a recipe for a successful partnership, it can present opportunities for collaboration and sharing resources that benefit both institutions and the children they serve.

Afterschool program staff and university faculty were often greeted with skepticism by public school teachers who were already highly stressed with the demand of their jobs and thus reluctant to spend time discussing student progress. However, the common ground theory worked with school staff. Parents granted permission for afterschool program staff to review and discuss school records so that school staff could have some confidence that everyone was working to support the student. A second important factor was that afterschool programs had to meet their professed goals of assisting students in completing their homework, working on projects, and studying for tests. The tutors were active in their academic support for the children in their program, and teachers were able to observe quickly the results of their efforts and appreciate that, finally, they had a supporting resource that would enhance their tremendous efforts. At this point, it is often possible to have extensive conversations about other skill support areas that the afterschool program can work on with their youth participants. Teachers and school administrators would make referrals to parents about the afterschool programs and the assistance they are able to provide, particularly for struggling students who lived in the neighborhood. Project staff were now seen as a significant source of support for the academic achievement of students. Teacher satisfaction with their afterschool program partners was evident in the end-of-year surveys completed by area teachers and is reflected in their comments below:

> She is an amazing student! This program has helped her grow even further academically and challenging her in ways I am not able to in the classroom.

> He is a great student and really blossoms when you work one-to-one with him. He *loves* all subjects and is like a sponge with retaining info/focus.

> She frequently comes to school and tells me stuff she's been studying about with her tutor. She likes to do little research projects about things her tutor has told her. She's developed interests in history and science. She also asks for homework about what we've been studying in math so she can do it with her tutor.

He has become more serious, is focusing better, and completing his assignments.

She has made great strides this school year. Her reading has improved dramatically and her overall attitude about school has changed. She has been an absolute joy to teach.

He has done much better academically as the school year has continued. Having someone to work with him one-to-one on his homework has been great because he is not getting it at home. Keep up the good work! He has benefited greatly from the program.

Problem Solving, Advice, and Consent

Problem-solving required significant community awareness, respect for community norms, and tolerance for an often fluid negotiating environment. Since the program involved both formal and informal contractual agreements, the first question was: whose role would it be to solve this issue? Again, open support from the community affairs staff was critical in working through this stage. A second question was: what actions were necessary to solve the problem? HOPE was in the unusual position of backing the CBOs' management and also advising and consulting about which strategies might be most successful. Although sometimes difficult, it became clear over time that the advisory role was effective, giving CBOs the space to determine what strategies were going to produce the desired outcomes for their organization and thus be more likely to be sustained. Resistance to advice or changes was an opportunity for negotiation or a period of trial-and-error where a particular strategy was implemented to see if it would work. If the pilot effort didn't work out, then that became the next focus of discussion. It was helpful to have had a process orientation with program development that gave more room for program differences and was respectful of partner ideas and experiences.

Financial and Contractual Arrangements

Another tension point that required diligent attention was careful financial distribution and contractual arrangements. Contracts, while necessarily formal, were essential for clarifying mutual responsibilities, reporting requirements, and deadlines. They also brought some objectivity to the relationship, stating from the outset that this was a partnership agreed to by both parties and which could be continued or ended. The formalities of reviewing, signing, and renewing contractual agreements ultimately added clarity and brought stability to partner relationships.

Many issues can quickly become contentious and a source of concern. Distribution arrangements needed to be fairly constructed and clearly managed. Inevitably, even with the best arrangements in place, problems in implementation arose. Having a responsive problem-solving attitude and making alternate arrangements when necessary was more effective than blaming or being rigid with partners. Assisting partners in complying with routine fiscal reporting arrangements (invoicing, auditing, and budgeting) supported the capacity-building infrastructure of the CBOs.

SUMMARY

Ultimately, the outcome of collaborative partnerships has proven to be worth the effort and resources it takes to sustain them. Project HOPE maintained a continuous data-gathering framework that demonstrated positive student outcomes as a result of participation in the afterschool programs. These data are summarized in Table 2.2.

Tracking student and program outcomes each year allowed everyone involved with the project to assess program improvements and growth.

TABLE 2.2. Project HOPE Changes Table, 2002–2009

	Year 1	Year 2	Year 3	Year 4	Year 5	Year 6	Year 7
Number of Sites	3	5	6	6	6	6	6
Number of Students	102	155	157	161	164	181	204
Student Return Rate	N/A	51%	54%	53%	43%	44%	64%
Average Program Attendance	62%	74%	81%	80%	81%	91%	92%
Report Card Collection	44%	60%	84%	96%	98%	90%	95%
Students with a C Average or Higher	72%	80%	74%	70%	82%	86%	91%
Students with a B Average or Higher	n/a	n/a	n/a	n/a	n/a	59%	76%
Number of Tutors	138	176	164	136	145	159	169
Tutor Return Rate	n/a	19%	27%	36%	18%	58%	n/a
Staff Return Rate	67% (4/6)	69% (9/13)	77% (10/13)	43% (6/14)	73% (11/15)	69% (9/13)	92% (12/13)

It also provided an incentive for program staff to find out what other programs were doing to improve their results. A simple changes table such as the one in Table 2.2 provided a snapshot for external personnel to get a quick sense of how programs were doing and to observe the steady improvement of student participants.

An additional benefit was that joint project administration had a normalizing impact on communication and relationships between partnership members. The frequent communication, networking, and respectful relationships built from implementing programs were only the beginning. The creation of supportive administrative and financial arrangements was critical to program success and sustainability. This required a commitment to improving the infrastructure of partner organizations that is often beyond the scope of afterschool program collaborative partnerships. Maintaining the collaborative partnership required staff who were dedicated to the tasks of program administration. The informal structures of collaborative partnerships benefited from the daily/weekly interactions that were a necessary component of specific jobs.

A positive and creative synergy can be created that naturally leads to program expansion, consultation with other programs, contact with agencies to initiate additional programs, and the dissemination of ideas throughout the networked communities. Good relations become fertile ground for developments that could not be foreseen during the original project design and implementation phase. The virtuous cycle created by such activities can lead to the frequent release of tensions and can contribute to the joint satisfaction that comes from a task well done. Indeed, doing together is far better than doing alone.

Lessons Learned: University and Community Partner Program Administration

- Define areas of control for each collaborative partner.
- Clarify roles and responsibilities for optimum effectiveness.
- Ensure that service delivery—the primary need for most community partners—is actively and consistently applied.
- Learn to listen and respond.
- Maintain regular contact with classroom teachers.
- Address student difficulties in a positive, responsive manner.
- Assist parents in resolving classroom concerns.
- Use formal agreements to reinforce program infrastructure.
- Be present in the work—try to understand the tensions and issues of concern and work to address them respectfully and promptly.

CHAPTER 3

Who Learns?

Experience enhances understanding: Understanding leads to more effective action. Both learning and service gain value and are transformed when combined in the specific types of activities we call service-learning.

—Eyler & Giles, *Where's the Learning in Service Learning?*

The importance of tutoring, mentoring, and shared activities in positive youth development is reported throughout the afterschool program literature. Garner (2002) describes several afterschool programs that utilize similar university and community programming partnerships that benefit community youths, such as literacy clubs, science learning programming, and computer education. Mahoney, Eccles, and Larson (2004) argue for the significant role of afterschool programs in promoting positive youth development, particularly minority youth. They present opportunities for building supportive relationships; belonging to a social environment and learning positive social norms; skill building; and promoting the integration of family, school, and community efforts. Halpern (2003) reinforces the significant role afterschool programs play in providing enrichment activities that draw students into the wider community environment. Students exhibit growing confidence in their school environment and greater familiarity with supporting educative institutions in their community.

Dr. David Malone, the current director of the Office of Service Learning, described early student involvement as a critical element in the development of service learning at Duke University. Student energy and enthusiasm led to the early organization of LEAPS (Learning through Experience, Action, Partnership, and Service), a peer mentoring program that added to the plethora of available tutoring programs, community service outreach projects, and service-learning coursework. Dr. Sam Miglarese, director of Community Engagement in the Office of Community Affairs, observed that students have the capacity to directly influence service-learning development on college campuses. He states that their dynamic engagement drives their ability to connect and engender in a tutee a newfound enthusiasm for academics or new pursuits such as taking a dive into the deep end of a pool for the first time. Faculty and staff efforts are necessary to ground the tutors' work in the deeper learning of coursework, program development, and the search for funding resources. Duke students working with Duke faculty and staff helped transform Duke's modest goals of working to improve local neighborhoods into the broader strategic goal of "knowledge in the service of society."

Through the groundbreaking efforts in the late 1990s of Rev. Betsy Alden, Duke's first director of the Office of Service Learning, consistent efforts were made to infuse service into the undergraduate coursework at Duke University. In the beginning, this was accomplished primarily with professors who already had field experience or who had participated in a program that could be modified to include a field-based experience. Departments such as education, psychology, sociology, and public policy developed this initial coursework. In 2002, the Kenan Institute for Ethics and the Hart Leadership Program (Sanford Institute of Public Policy) were awarded a 3-year Fund for Improvement of Postsecondary Education grant to further integrate service learning into the undergraduate curriculum. In combination with a small amount of civic engagement funding from Project HOPE, these two grants were key to providing the initial resources for civic engagement development at Duke University. The Fund for Improvement of Postsecondary Education grant, directed by Elisabeth Kiss (now president of Agnes Scott College) and Alma Blount (director of the Hart Leadership Program at Duke), gave faculty the resources that enabled them to think carefully about developing undergraduate pathways to deepen student engagement and integrate service with coursework disciplines.

Project HOPE operated in full partnership with the Office of Service Learning and the Fund for Improvement of Postsecondary Education grant course pathways development project. HOPE staff worked with the conviction that quality university engagement that focused on community needs would be of mutual benefit to both the community and the university. For this to happen, it was important that university activities provide direct services to community partner organizations and significant learning opportunities for afterschool students, university students, community partners, and university faculty and staff. Promoting positive youth development for Durham's school-aged minority youth was the primary goal of the community-based afterschool programs and university partners. Involving Duke undergraduates with afterschool students in tutoring and mentoring activities seemed a logical match that would be of mutual benefit to the community and the university. The development and implementation of a program that met the dual goals of promoting academic achievement among low-income minority students and improving the learning experiences of Duke undergraduates presented challenges and significant opportunities for Project HOPE administrators.

Rev. Betsy Alden met early and often with Project HOPE staff to ensure that the project was grounded in service-learning principles. Rev. Alden had come to Duke University with a rich background of service-learning development in prior university settings and was a recognized national leader in the field. Along with Dr. David Malone, she had designed the civic engagement component of the Kellogg grant so that adequate resources were available for the coursework and personnel support that was necessary to effectively implement the service and education coursework development. Dr. Malone also worked closely with Project HOPE staff to develop the service-learning framework for the afterschool programs. Service learning in this context was defined as

> a course-based, credit-bearing educational experience in which students a) participate in an organized service activity that meets identified community needs and b) reflect on the service activity in such a way as to gain further understanding of course content, a broader appreciation of the discipline, and an enhanced sense of civic responsibility. (Bringle & Hatcher, 1999, p. 179)

Service learning is grounded in John Dewey's educational philosophy, which can be expressed in three basic principles: (a) education must lead to personal growth, (b) education must contribute to humane conditions, and (c) education must engage citizens in association with one another (Bringle & Hatcher, 1999). For university students, the benefits of quality service-learning experiences often transform their personal and professional lives. They move from passive participants in college classrooms to active community members who are engaged and intent on solving complex problems in situational contexts. They are addressing authentic problems, raising significant questions, and having a daily impact on the lives of their communities. Static knowledge and theoretical constructs are tested in real-world circumstances, creating meaningful learning, practical skills, and habits of community activism. Students are directly involved in addressing pressing community needs and, in the process, are supporting their community. They will continue to apply their gained knowledge and skills in their future communities. The goals of integrated learning are articulated by Ramaley (2007) in her reflective article in the *Wingspread Journal*:

> The goal of engaged scholarship is not to define and serve the public good directly *on behalf* of society, but to create conditions for the public good to be interpreted and pursued in a collaborative mode *with* the community. In contemporary society, the exercise of citizenship requires constant learning and the thoughtful and ethical application of knowledge. By including our students in *engaged* scholarship, we introduce them to basic concepts and, at the same time, offer them a chance to explore the application and consequences of ideas in the company of mature scholars and practitioners. By drawing inspiration from our community connections, we enrich our own lives as scholars and teachers and together ensure that society will have the knowledge and insights that it will need to remain healthy and competitive in a changing world order. (p. 10)

Fortunately for Project HOPE staff, Dr. Malone had developed model service-learning coursework in the Program in Education at Duke University during the 1990s. Duke students taking his courses were involved in tutoring Durham Public School students in the five elementary schools located in the Duke–Durham Neighborhood Partnership. This tutoring program, Partners for Success, provided the basic tutoring model for the afterschool programs as well. Students enrolled in education courses were required to fulfill 20 service-learning hours tutoring in either the public schools or afterschool programs. As the quality of the afterschool programs improved, additional education faculty became comfortable with their students also tutoring in both the school and afterschool settings. Currently, the majority of courses taught in the Program in Education have a strong service-learning component. Dr. Jan Riggsbee, the current director of the Program in Education, views service learning as a critical component in the teacher-training program. Future teachers gain direct experience in developing civic engagement activities as an integrated element of the curriculum. As a teaching strategy, service learning enhances student content learning and also engages students in solving pressing community problems.

Duke University's education faculty are also strong advocates for service-learning pedagogy within the broader university community. In 2008, the university's Office of Service Learning, which supports all Duke faculty who teach service-learning courses, was moved to the

Program in Education. Through this office, Duke faculty and staff have created a service-learning support network that provides learning opportunities and resources to faculty members who are teaching or interested in teaching service-learning courses in their respective disciplines.

Although predominantly an academic exercise, service learning must also benefit community partners. Successful service-learning experiences require coordinated partnerships between the campus and the community. As Project HOPE began its work with community partners, they expressed concerns that undergraduate tutors were often not dependable or particularly well-trained. Developing the service-learning framework created an improved learning environment for afterschool students and their Duke tutors. Duke tutors received the training and monitoring they needed to become more effective tutors. As a result of this improved structure, afterschool students received individual attention, direct academic support, and critical social skills necessary for sustained academic achievement. Community partners benefited from consistent volunteer assistance in their programs throughout the year and resource development from university project staff. Finally, all participants benefited from the reciprocal learning and improved connections of working together over a sustained period at an urgently needed task—creating a positive learning environment and enrichment opportunities for Durham's students. The following narrative describes in greater detail the learning experiences of the afterschool students, Duke undergraduate tutors, community partners, and Duke faculty and staff.

AFTERSCHOOL PARTICIPANTS

> African-American children are the proxy for what ails American education in general. And so, as we fashion solutions which help African-American children, we fashion solutions which help all children.
> —Augustus F. Hawkins, in Tucker & Herman,
> "Using Culturally Sensitive Theories and Research to Meet the
> Academic Needs of Low-Income African-American Children"

Durham school-aged youth present a lively and engaging picture. Who wouldn't want to work with these bright, promising young people? They are open, loving, funny, loud, challenging, energetic, restless, and curious budding poets, artists, scientists. Sit down in any afterschool program chair as a guest and soon you will be a participant, asked to read a book, work on a homework assignment, play a game, help out with snacks, share a joke or resolve an altercation. The promise and challenge of our young people comes rushing at you and invites you to join the struggle; it is life itself. Baseline data on the afterschool students presented an all-too-familiar profile of minority youth, predominantly African American, aged 5–18. Test scores were stubbornly sitting at a below 50% passing rate, afterschool program attendance was irregular, and communication with school personnel infrequent. Students were struggling and parents and community members were concerned and committed to helping their children do better academically and socially. Community partners often expressed frustration with a public school system that they felt was unresponsive to the needs of minority youth. They were anxious to develop afterschool programs that would support the school-aged children of their communities. Table 3.1 describes the demographic participation in Project HOPE over its 7-year history. There are no formal enrollment criteria for the program, so the evenness in the male/female ratio and age ranges over the scope of the project is a random result of student and parent choices.

Since the mid-1990s, Duke undergraduate tutors working in the Durham Public Schools indicated positive results from their tutoring and mentoring experience. Duke faculty and community partners decided to launch a pilot program having Duke tutors work in the afterschool program setting, hypothesizing that the experience, if properly structured, would support the academic achievement of the low-income minority children who were struggling in the public school system. Over the next 7 years, the results of the program confirmed this initial positive planning, with Durham school-age students demonstrating improved program attendance, report card grades, and rising end-of-grade test scores. Participant surveys conducted during this time frame indicated consistently positive attitudes toward the afterschool program, its tutors, and the students' respective schools.

Alongside these more formal outcomes, less formal but equally important social outcomes could be observed in the developing tutoring relationships. Because tutoring occurred in the community-based afterschool programs, the community youth were operating from *their* base, a place of psychological and physical safety. It was their home, their cultural norms and practices, and their community relationships. Initially, the tutors were guests who were forced to negotiate an unfamiliar cultural landscape, but who came with important skills to offer. The terms had to be negotiated before significant engagement and work would happen. This was a frequent difficulty for the tutors, who had to

TABLE 3.1. Community Center Demographics, 2002–2008

Ethnicity Distribution of Students Enrolled in Community Centers	02–03	03–04	04–05	05–06	06–07	07–08	08–09	Total
African American	100	156	136	139	143	152	171	997
Hispanic	2	6	16	15	19	23	29	110
Caucasian	0	3	2	5	2	6	4	22
Other	0	1	3	2	0	0	0	6
Total	102	166	157	161	164	181	204	1135

Gender Distribution of Students Enrolled in Community Centers	02–03	03–04	04–05	05–06	06–07	07–08	08–09	Total
Female	57	81	83	85	88	106	106	606
Male	45	85	74	76	76	75	98	529
Total	102	166	157	161	164	181	204	1135

Age Distribution of Students Enrolled in Community Centers	02–03	03–04	04–05	05–06	06–07	07–08	08–09	Total
4–7 years	15	32	15	23	47	52	59	243
8–10 years	30	67	50	46	59	90	96	438
11–13 years	34	40	51	64	45	34	45	313
14–17 years	17	17	18	28	13	5	4	102
Age Unknown	6	10	23	0	0	0	0	39
Total	102	166	157	161	164	181	204	1135

Grade Distribution of Students Enrolled in Community Centers	02–03	03–04	04–05	05–06	06–07	07–08	08–09	Total
Pre-K	0	0	6	2	1	2	0	11
Kindergarten	5	9	5	11	11	14	17	72
Grade 1	5	11	10	16	17	11	16	86
Grade 2	7	13	15	8	19	26	23	111
Grade 3	16	23	33	25	18	33	37	185
Grade 4	8	31	24	16	29	30	36	174
Grade 5	10	20	26	26	15	33	27	157
Grade 6	10	14	13	25	18	12	26	104
Grade 7	10	13	9	18	23	10	14	97
Grade 8	12	12	2	4	7	7	4	51
Grade 9	3	7	6	4	1	1	3	23
Grade 10	6	2	1	2	3	0	0	14
Grade 11	1	3	2	3	0	2	1	13
Grade 12	0	0	1	1	2	0	0	4
Grade Unknown	9	8	4	0	0	0	0	21
Total	102	166	157	161	164	181	204	1135

learn that building a trusting relationship with their students must come before learning could occur. Duke students expressed their growing understanding of building relationships as a critical element that supported student learning:

> I realized that you must develop a relationship with a student before you are able to teach them anything that they will actually understand.

> I have found that relating to and reaching out to a student is so essential to get him or her to learn and to have the motivation to learn. No matter age, race, class, or gender, once you learn about a child and get to know his or her interests and incorporate these into the lessons, it is so much easier to teach! And more fun for both of you!

Work habits and study skills were introduced, reinforced, and extended over time. The afterschool programs struggled to develop "study zone" expectations, structuring time frames and spaces where work would happen on a daily basis. Some programs were more successful than others, but all the programs were able to improve their study zone practices. Tutors learned to balance activities, games, and structured learning appropriate to the needs of their individual students. This might involve conventional strategies such as flash cards, word banks, and reading comprehension exercises as well as board games and journal or poetry writing. Math evolved from worksheets to manipulatives, flash cards, reinforcing math games, multiplication jump rope, and teaching Cartesian coordinates through playing football.

A predominant theme was that work habits and study yielded positive results. Study skills were reinforced daily by tutors modeling appropriate work-habit behaviors, providing critical social modeling for afterschool program participants. Social modeling by the tutors was multifaceted. Work-habit behaviors involved students and tutors showing up regularly and on time, organizing themselves into a productive work period with appropriate work tasks, and using positively reinforcing statements and activities that emphasized growing competence. Mastery and confidence with academic tasks revealed that there was no mystery to school success, and academic challenges yielded to applied study habits. Competence was further reinforced by earned praise for task accomplishments, improved grades, and school performance. By 2008–2009, 91% of Project HOPE students maintained a C average or better on their report cards, and 76% of HOPE students maintained a B average on their report cards.

Tutors and afterschool program staff who observe these steps have an important function of providing a supportive social construct. Their assistance in regularly negotiating school concerns as they arise prevents the creation of larger problems that are harder to resolve. Working daily alongside their peers in the afterschool program, they create a supportive social group that provides additional support to students as they move from the community to the school setting.

The community afterschool program also offered cultural grounding to its youth through cultural transmission. This was done through guest speakers from the community, participation in community cultural events, and celebrations that reinforced community values and pride. The HOPE afterschool program collaborated with university and community partners on oral history projects, documentary filming, photographic history exhibits, and informal sharing by community members about their experiences growing up in the neighborhood. Durham has a rich African American community history that has been documented through books, films, and photographs. Community celebrations, lectures, and events that informed and invited students to engage in that history were an important element of the afterschool programs' resources.

In addition to this specific cultural grounding, afterschool programs provided the means to explore and express personal interests through a variety of activities and resources. Although each center may not have the resources to provide a full range of activities, each developed activities and resources that were suited to its capacities. Physical activities were routinely popular, some being informal in nature such as pickup or one-on-one basketball games, jump rope games, walks to neighborhood parks, or field trips to regional parks, swimming pools, bowling alleys, or skating rinks. More formal skill-based physical activities such as swim lessons, tennis lessons, and basketball or soccer games were developed through volunteer activities organized by university or recreation sports teams. Through performances, workshops, or residences, visiting artists reinforced language arts through drama, poetry, and writing activities. Dance and music workshops sparked student interest, taught skills, and provided outlets for creative expression. Again, university student volunteers were important here, providing interactive science and health lessons, arts and crafts workshops, and recreation activities. Tickets to movies, athletic events, community and university performances, and cultural events widened the social and cultural world of community youth.

Throughout the first 5 years of the Project HOPE centers, the resource implementation process was critical in supporting Durham youth development and the exercise of their physical and creative talents. A host of role models from the community, university, and wider adult world became involved with Durham community youth on a regular basis. Prior to the DDNP, many youth had never been on Duke University's campus. Durham youth now have significantly increased opportunities to participate in campus activities and use campus facilities. Programs such as Swim with the Blue Devils, Tennis Club, WOODS (outdoor science lessons), and Woodsmont are examples of this improved resource access. The resources chart in Chapter 2 (Table 2.1) gives a realistic picture of how university resources were able to become a part of integrated service delivery to Project HOPE afterschool programs. Anecdotal testimony from site coordinators has included observations such as noticing that children are now swimming in the pool during sessions, whereas in past years they may have only sat beside the pool. Many students now travel routinely by bus or train to regional and national parks and museums, even going on educational trips to places as far away as Washington, DC, Atlanta, New York City, Baltimore, and Orlando.

In summary, what do afterschool students learn? From their tutors, they learn specific academic skills that can range from improved reading and math skills to writing as creative expression, science as an area of curiosity and exploration, and history as a source of civic pride and engagement. Habits of learning are taught and reinforced by the tutoring and less-formal afterschool program structure, including regular attendance, a disciplined work schedule, on-time task completion, and a sense of accomplishment and competency. Working with others, getting support when needed, and peer collaboration are a part of the afterschool program structure, resulting in a sense of community and support across cultures.

The results of surveys administered to elementary and secondary students are consistently positive in their evaluation of students' interest in school and learning and their expectation that they will complete high school and continue to college or other postsecondary training. Setting these goals early and reinforcing them consistently through the adolescent years is critical for positive youth development. Afterschool programs are a critical mediating and complementary learning space for reinforcing these academic and social objectives.

Students completing the surveys indicated high levels of satisfaction with the program, noting that they enjoyed having a tutor and getting help, playing games when they were done with their work, working on the computers, and going on field trips. Survey results are discussed in more detail in Chapter 4. Average program attendance of 91–92% for the last 2 years and over 80% for the last 5 years indicates overall student satisfaction with the afterschool programs. The following student comments are typical of what the afterschool participants say about their tutors:

> I like having a tutor because the things I do with my tutor I don't get to do with my teacher.

> I feel very happy to have tutor so that she can teacher me somethings and learn more and pass my grade.

> I am doing better than I used to before I had a tutor. I am doing better in school.

UNIVERSITY STUDENTS

I have learned lessons about life that I will carry with me for the rest of my life. I have realized the importance of patience in my time working with my tutee. This was a character trait that was lacking before my experience at EK Powe. I have also learned that tutors' impacts on their students can be profound and truly meaningful. Working with him has once again opened my heart and eyes up to just how special young children are and the responsibility that adults must accept to educate these invaluable individuals.
—Response from an anonymous Duke student service-learning survey

When university students begin the tutoring process, they often see themselves as competent individuals fully capable of promoting the academic success of the students they are assigned to tutor. As they confront the challenges of the tutoring experience and discover how much they have to learn about the teaching process, real applied learning can begin. Tutors enter the experience along a wide continuum of prior educational background and experiences. When training and supervising tutors, it's important to keep this continuum in mind so that it's possible to reinforce the learning that needs to take place for each incoming tutor to be effective. Tutors also have to work on their match with the student they are teaching. This involves analyzing the tutor's knowledge base and skills and determining how well they coordinate with what the student being tutored actually needs. Tutors need to know that they do not have all the answers and that they can expect to make mistakes. They may struggle and be confused as they work through the first challenges of the tutoring experience:

- *The amount of energy and effort required in teaching.* "If you are not up to the task, it is better for the student and yourself that you avoid becoming a teacher."
- *Problem solving.* "I had to find new ways to understand things my tutee was learning and develop different ways to teach it to him and make it fun and understandable."
- *Working with others and finding different ways to reach different people.* "Things did not always work, so I had to improvise and try new things."

For all of these reasons, it becomes important to design and implement a tutoring experience infrastructure that supports the tutor learning process as effectively as the learning experience for the afterschool student participant. The service-learning experience was originally designed as preservice fieldwork preparing Duke undergraduate students for teaching licensure. However, it's important to note that the education program at Duke allows nonlicensure students to take its primary introductory education courses. This allows students who are not strictly education licensure candidates to participate in education courses and gives a broad cross-section of Duke students knowledge of education issues and challenges. Education faculty were committed to assisting the development of new teachers through exposing them to realistic teaching experiences in order to better prepare them for their future classroom experiences. They also wanted nonlicensure students to experience the real world of teaching and learning in diverse education environments with a multicultural student body. The service-learning experience, which integrates undergraduate coursework with tutoring field practice, gives the tutoring experience an ongoing supportive framework.

Faculty worked with a full-time service-learning coordinator to implement the infrastructure needed to support several hundred undergraduate tutors working in neighborhood schools and afterschool programs during the semester. The service-learning coordinator organized the placement of each tutor based on the needs of the afterschool program sites and their match with tutor interests and semester schedules. An intensive tutor orientation covering topics such as literacy and math training, behavior management, and diversity issues was held early in each semester. Once the tutors were placed in their sites, the service-learning coordinator visited the sites on a weekly or biweekly basis throughout the semester in order to monitor and trouble-shoot any concerns. The service-learning coordinator also continuously provided the site coordinators and tutors with instructional resources and advice throughout the semester. The service-learning coordinator participated in monthly afterschool program meetings and also with service-learning faculty as necessary throughout the semester. Data on tutor demographics, tutor hours, and tutor feedback was collected and analyzed by the service-learning coordinator and shared with faculty and afterschool program administrators.

Through their coursework, undergraduates learned core educational, learning, and motivational concepts, which they were able to apply in their tutoring field practice. Through this process, they saw for themselves whether the course constructs were effective. Written reflections and course papers, class discussions, and projects provided ample opportunities to raise issues and to further explore and strengthen their intellectual engagement. University undergraduates may or may not have had prior experience with tutoring, working within the community center environment, or working across cultural boundaries. For some students, tutoring may be their first direct experience with socioeconomic inequities and their impact on the lives of children. Other students may have read or understood intellectually existing economic and social issues, but giving these problems a real face would have a significant impact on their understanding and thinking about these issues.

Continuous monitoring by university program staff became a safety net for the tutors as they moved through this learning process. For many students, this is an introduction to the process of learning. They reflect on how they learn best and what study habits have been most effective for themselves. This process occurs parallel to working with their student, learning how another person learns best. It may be similar to theirs or it may be different, forcing the tutors to become flexible in their applied learning strategies. University teams of faculty and staff read written reflection logs and papers to individually address learning and tutoring issues as they emerge.

Cross-cultural issues and tension points arise at least as often as academic concerns. These issues can be as basic as university tutors struggling to comply with community center dress codes and courtesy requirements. The predominantly African American site staff expected to be addressed formally (unless they gave tutors permission to do otherwise) and with respect. In contrast, tutors entering an afterschool program may be nervous or too casual in their attire and demeanor. Religion was often integrated into the daily life of afterschool programs, with prayer circle times, grace said before meals, and visits from the minister or other church and community volunteers. Tutors coming from a variety of socioeconomic and social backgrounds may or may not be comfortable with these social practices. Disciplinary management often required adjustments with site coordinators, who were stricter and more direct in their behavioral expectations of the students than the tutors. Tutors frequently needed time to observe, understand, and develop a comfortable management style that would coexist with center expectations.

> *Discipline and motivation*: Naturally an easygoing, soft sort of person, I had to toughen up my prior discipline tactics in order to be effective. Speaking firmly and showing with my eyes that I meant business really produced results.

> I think the biggest thing for me that the field experience helped me understand is the different styles and philosophies of learning and trying them out and seeing what works best. I was lucky and school came easily to me, but for my tutee, I had to change around and try new things to really get her to learn and like learning.

Tutors came to know that they belonged socially to the community centers as they shared meals and activities at the center and learned about the families and neighborhood. As tutors became more relaxed and comfortable in the community centers, they emerged from the semester with an expanded comfort zone, which gave them greater freedom and knowledge to operate in expanded classroom and community environments. Often they started their own volunteer programs addressing a particular area of study. Examples of student groups that have operated independently in the afterschool programs are WOODS (science and outdoor recreation), Arts Connect (art instruction), and Club Tennis (tennis lessons).

What do university students learn from their tutoring and service-learning experiences? They learn to bridge theory and practice as basic learning principles. Through class readings and discussions they learn theoretical constructs that can then be applied experientially. The learning is thus reinforced and becomes a better integrated learning experience. Tutors learn practical strategies that they can apply constructively in other settings. These include basic teaching practices such as lesson planning, task analysis for teaching academic skills, and some fundamental behavior management techniques. Depending on their social backgrounds, students develop expanded cultural competencies, which may involve exposure to students from different ethnic, socioeconomic, or religious backgrounds. Tutors may be exposed to students with disabilities or students who are struggling with proper nutrition or difficult family circumstances. Students frequently comment in the postsemester survey that they have learned as much or more than the students they tutored.

> The academic part of the course gave me a chance to clarify my own ideas in a broader intellectual context. The service learning allowed me to apply those ideas, and ultimately I had an amazingly rewarding experience—and I intend to maintain a relationship with my students in the future.

> It's shocking how directly applicable all the theories we discussed are to schooling. There isn't as much of a direct correspondence in other fields. When we discussed a new concept in class, I could go tutor and see it in play the very same day.

SCHOOL SYSTEM

> She frequently comes to school and tells me stuff she's been studying about with her tutor. She likes to do little research projects about things her tutor has told her. She's developed interests in history and science. She also asks for homework about what we've been studying in math so she can do it with her tutor.
> —Teacher survey comments, 2009

School system personnel and afterschool personnel often co-exist in uneasy collaborative relationships. Burdened classroom teachers do not have the time and energy to communicate regularly with afterschool program personnel about daily homework assignments, upcoming quizzes, tests, and projects. Providing aligned instructional materials, textbooks, and specific instructional areas for students who need tutoring assistance can seem an overwhelming task for many classroom teachers and school administrators.

Afterschool program staff can become equally frustrated as they attempt to work with students from different classrooms and schools. Students are often resistant to doing homework, are disorganized, and are careless about bringing home the necessary information about their assignments and instructional tasks. Any adult who has puzzled over incomprehensible worksheets, projects due the next day, or upcoming tests knows a fraction of the frustration that afterschool personnel face every day.

Successful afterschool programs work hard to bridge this gap between schools and the afterschool programs. The task is easier if the program is located directly in the school, with afterschool program staff potentially having easier access to teachers and school resources. Staff may be drawn directly from the teaching and paraprofessional school staff, which gives them an advantage in understanding the student homework tasks. For community-based afterschool programs, however, it is necessary to designate staff that can regularly maintain contact with school system personnel.

By its third year, Project HOPE found that it needed a full-time liaison coordinator to work with the school system. The liaison coordinator organized basic school information on a consistent basis for the afterschool site coordinators in order to ensure their inclusion in the continuous problem-solving feedback loop. This information could be as simple as sharing the school calendar or as complex as analyzing report card grades and end-of-grade test results. Once this relationship was established, afterschool program site coordinators and university project staff were able to share the information that they had gathered about what might be happening in the public school system. Examples of this would be parent workshops on providing homework help, transitioning to middle or high school, summer camp information, and community events.

Because the liaison coordinator is often responsible for working with as many as 35–40 schools during the academic year, the coordination framework for teachers is individualized. Each teacher of an afterschool program student receives a letter in late September or early October informing them that a student in their class is also participating in a HOPE afterschool program. The liaison coordinator also visits the schools and introduces herself to the faculty and office personnel. At this time, the liaison coordinator shares with school personnel parent permission letters giving her the authority to discuss student progress with teachers and to access Individual Education Plans, report cards, and end-of-grade testing data. In addition, she circulates her contact information and lets the school staff know that she's available to discuss student concerns as they emerge over the school year. However, at this point, all of these important preparatory arrangements are just good intentions. For the framework to be effective, communication strategies that support student achievement are necessary throughout the school year.

Experience taught HOPE project staff quickly that getting access to the *first* report card was essential to providing the necessary support to any student that might be struggling. In Durham Public Schools, there is a central reporting system for the secondary schools, but no similar system for the elementary schools. As a consequence, for elementary students, each teacher must be contacted for their report card records. As a practical matter, the liaison coordinator, therefore, worked closely with each afterschool program coordinator to collect as many report cards as possible from their students. The report card collection percentages were documented and celebrated at the monthly afterschool coordinator meetings. In the early years, the report collection rates were below 50%; in contrast, the more recent average collection rate was 93%. This successful report card collection rate meant that afterschool program site coordinators had quick and sustained access to information from teachers about student attendance, academic progress, and behavioral issues.

The liaison coordinator was then able to review report cards and note students who were experiencing difficulties. Follow-up visits to the classroom teachers of struggling students provided further information about what difficulties students were experiencing and to get teacher feedback on strategies for improving student work. This targeted approach gave direct assistance to students, teachers, and the afterschool coordinators and tutors. Parents were able to talk more confidentially with teachers and afterschool program coordinators because they had more information about what was happening in the classroom. As a further reinforcing communication device, the liaison coordinator developed a one-page Individual Student Plan that contained report card and test score data for each student in the DDNP afterschool program. As teachers worked with the liaison coordinator to identify skill areas that needed to be strengthened, this information was entered on the Individual Student Plan. The updated Individual Student Plan and report card information were shared with the coordinators and tutors and then kept on file at the afterschool program site.

Communication patterns were thus established, and operated continuously throughout the school year. As afterschool program site coordinators become aware of family issues or situational concerns, the liaison coordinator shared this interpersonal information with school staff. Typical issues which have arisen are health concerns, deaths in the family, custody shifts, and job changes or moves. The two-way communication patterns often shifted from formal to informal, allowing for more information to be shared effectively. Parents were included in this loop, which worked to minimize their frustration with school staff.

A final note on this interaction is necessary. Teachers who are able to interact positively with afterschool program staff receive additional critical support from community members in their efforts to reach and teach children. This assists teachers as an additional means of bridging the cultural divide that can exist between the social institution of school and minority communities. Relationships built around the common ground of improving the academic and social achievement of school-aged minority youth are significant factors in positive youth development. Youth that are engaged with their school communities develop healthier and more varied activity involvement. This is a benefit for minority youth development and their communities (Vandell & Pierce, 2002).

COMMUNITY PARTNERS

> First, the heart is far more important than the head. Lots of efforts are head efforts. Lots of things have money, expertise, they have this and that and everything else, but they don't have any heart. Anybody on the street can read that. If there isn't any heart to it, then the head doesn't even matter.
>
> —Medoff & Sklar, *Streets of Hope*

Community partners and CBOs bring a special skill set to the community and university partnership. Community partners and their afterschool program staff are often recognized leaders in their respective community and longtime residents of the community. As such, they share the ethnic identities, common experiences, and values of the neighborhoods they represent. Often, they know the children and the families of the children in the afterschool program personally. This can ease initial communication and contact patterns. The coordinators of the programs also possess professional skills that can be representative of the career and employment opportunities available to afterschool program students. These skill sets may involve college education, professional certification as teachers and administrators, civil service experiences, and community or social entrepreneurship. As community leaders, they have the ability to explain and model the skills and community norms necessary to negotiate wider social networks and institutions (Hirsch, 2005). Parents and students often are more willing to discuss issues and problems with them because there is a degree of psychological safety that comes from shared culture and experiences. The coordinators and staff also provide a vital link in being able to explain circumstances to university faculty and staff in ways that they can understand as well as performing a critical bridging function through the program administration process (Cooper, Denner, & Lopez, 1999).

Working with university faculty and staff as well as community partners who are administering similar programs presents unique learning opportunities for community partners and their organizations. While representing their own neighborhood's interest, community partners can have regular dialogue across accepted community boundaries with other community partners and CBOs. Regular interaction of this nature creates opportunities for developing joint advocacy around common issues and problems. Shared administration creates a loose network that can be used to advocate for funding and resources that would be less accessible to smaller organizations.

Community partners can also gain access to important logistical, financial, and evaluation resources through these shared program networks. Logistical support can include assistance with developing daily schedule, lesson planning, tutor training, and management support. Ongoing financial support is critical to the stabilization of most afterschool programming. Developing access to a wider, more diverse funding base can be an all-consuming task that few CBOs can sustain. University faculty and staff can often assist with grant writing, grant management, and access to other financial development resources that can assist significantly in easing this burden. Similarly, the documentation required for financial reporting as well as program documentation and development can be provided through university resources. Training along with field staff support can successfully implement the infrastructure development necessary for program sustainability.

As programs stabilize and develop, community partners can also attend training, workshops, and conferences to further develop their program management skills. These training needs can be diverse, but they might include: behavior management skills workshops; reading, math, or other academic skills training; and nonprofit management or development and fundraising skills training. Local and regional conferences can provide skills training as well as access to guest speakers and lecturers on relevant topics. The experience of participating in these training opportunities provides a shared opportunity to work with other participants and professional trainers who are engaged with similar issues. Common ground is built through this network of interactions.

Community center staff face many challenges in managing their roles and responsibilities as supervisors of a widely diverse range of children in afterschool programs. There is often high turnover in community center staff due to the part-time hours and low pay of this work. Although afterschool program staff may have college degrees and professional certification, supporting staff are often paraprofessionals with less education and training. As communities and universities increase their interest and development of afterschool programs there is a growing demand for improving and supporting the continuing education of afterschool program staff. The After School Corporation program in New York City reports that it has begun to establish community groups and university faculty who will be involved with for youth development professional training (Friedman & Bleiberg, 2002). The United Kingdom provides an example of a comprehension approach to afterschool program staff development with its ContinYou program. They have compiled a mapping report of accredited and noncredited training courses available to their afterschool program staff. Staff programming also exists to train community youth workers in beginning teacher-training courses at U.K. universities and colleges (Fordham, 2004).

An underlying social skill set is reinforced through this process, both for community partners among themselves and with university and community agency members. All too frequently, mistrust has built up within the community due to negative past experiences. This may be a result of prior slights and hurts, program ventures that have been attempted and failed, or distorted perceptions of the social "other." Having the opportunity for open communication as well as regular shared experiences provides multiple chances for trusting relationships to develop. This can be a delicate arena and needs persistent attention, humor, and honesty, sometimes at the cost of pride and ego.

UNIVERSITY FACULTY AND STAFF

Working with community partners from an advisor/partner role places university faculty and staff into a participant learner position as well. Acknowledging the asymmetrical nature of the university–community partnership requires university participants to develop a deliberate, collaborative working style that fosters consensual management practices whenever possible. The guest–host boundary is ever present and fluid and needs to be respected. The rewards come as the group's talents and skills emerge and the group develops the distinctive voice that is the project's own. Group strengths can then be optimized and weaknesses minimized through the collaborative effort.

Establishing clear communication patterns with community partners requires discussing common interests and goals openly with program management administration. This requires developing a degree of comfort with ceding areas of program administrative control to community partners. Heightened democratic administrative practices and increased program flexibility may be more difficult to implement with controlled research design formats. This impacts faculty research practices and grant administration. In addition, a focus on resisting the inclination to promise more than can be delivered can clarify the actual capabilities of the university program staff and the program's financial status. This is difficult because of the healthy impulse to want to do more for the project and the community. Providing reflective practice and feedback loops for the community partners can help everyone think about vital program improvement issues.

Working in the process of university and community partnerships requires both personal and professional flexibility. There will be conceptual boundary shifts because the afterschool program roles and responsibilities are not as rigid as they might be in a more typical school setting. It's much easier to become part of the programming flow, to interact with center staff and children, and to get drawn into program concerns and personnel issues. Similarly, learning new languages can be a requirement—this may involve knowledge of a second language such a Spanish to accommodate a growing Latino population, or it might be simply understanding the informal flow of language, songs, customs, and culture in the neighborhood. Neighborhoods are different, and there are cultural shifts that need to be accommodated as program staff moves from one neighborhood to another. Learning and appreciating community concerns and helping to express those concerns to a wider audience is one of the broad roles of university program staff. This can involve the management of difficult issues that require both honesty and humor from all parties.

Another area of learning for community partners, university students, and university faculty has been the area of community-based research and service learning. Afterschool programs and summer programs provide an excellent opportunity for university students to conduct research projects that are based on stated community center needs. Supervised by university faculty, students are able to design, implement, and complete research projects that extend their learning and training while also providing program assistance to the community center participants.

During its first year, Project HOPE worked with collaborating faculty and staff to develop the Duke–Durham Scholars program, which was a combination of learning internships and a follow-up intensive community-based research course that consistently produced community-based research projects. Examples of Duke–Durham Scholars projects included the development of nutrition workshops, social skills, tutor training, and civic engagement curriculums that were used in the community center summer programs. Other afterschool programs have documented similar experiences. For example, Hirsch (2005) describes a graduate research project on a gender equity initiative designed to promote sports programs for middle-school girls participating in Chicago area Boys and Girls Clubs. Students trained in these research techniques leave their university environments better able to conduct and refine the community-based research process.

Working with undergraduate and graduate students in conducting community-based research requires thinking differently about research. The often fluid, underfunded, and underresourced nature of many afterschool programs can make conducting research challenging for all partners involved. Using documentation and research techniques that have design flexibility and are less intrusive in the conduct of program activities may be a necessary requirement for research staff. These may include qualitative research techniques such as field observations, interviews, focus groups, field process notes, learning products (student journals, work samples, course papers), and surveys to gather project information. Keeping community partners well-informed through regular feedback and a usable final product can effectively promote positive research activities within community center settings.

SUMMARY

Within the collaborative learning systems context, multiple learning communities can be created that support the growth of all participants. The student participant in the afterschool program is firmly nested with peers and a variety of community adults who are engaged and invested with their well-being. Although there is no guarantee of success, the odds are substantially increased for positive youth development and improved communities.

Through their interaction with other afterschool program coordinators and university staff, community partners expand their knowledge and skills base. Coordinators gain greater curriculum and instructional resource knowledge, improved technology skills, and tutor and volunteer management skills.

University undergraduates who tutor afterschool program participants make substantial gains in their knowledge and skills. Academically, they become firmly grounded in the theoretical knowledge and practical application of the core concepts of their undergraduate coursework. As service-learning participants, they become more firmly connected with their communities and civically engaged in the community's improved outcomes. Fundamentally, they are firmly grounded in bridging ideas with realistic, practical applications and are developing the necessary tools for making a positive difference in society. Duke University has embraced the value of service learning for its undergraduates. This is evident in its support of the Office of Service Learning, which continues to expand the quantity and quality of service-learning courses and activities at Duke University. Concurrently, the university and the Gates Foundation are both funding DukeEngage, an international, national, and local civic engagement program designed to provide Duke undergraduates with expanded civic engagement opportunities locally, nationally, and globally.

University faculty and staff engaged in Project HOPE have developed a significantly more nuanced vision of community issues and concerns. They also have sustained deeper connections with multiple community partners. As a result of their repeated exposure and collaborative work with community partners, they are developing more effective research agendas and are working to direct funding efforts to more effective purposes.

Finally, the core group of afterschool students and their families, community partners, and university staff form a strong, positive advocacy group within the community. As the successful results of the university–community partnership become more broadly known and acknowledged, programs are poised for expansion in multiple contexts. Project HOPE staff have consistently worked with Durham Public Schools and North Carolina Central University to expand afterschool program opportunities within Durham. Durham Public Schools were recently awarded a grant from the 21st Century Community Learning Centers to develop after-school and summer learning programs in the housing projects adminis-tered by the Durham Housing Authority. In addition, selected elementary and middle schools also have active afterschool programs. The collective result of each of these efforts is expanded learning opportunities for low-income minority students in Durham.

Dissemination of ideas and lessons learned through community ad-vocacy, collaboration with other provider institutions, and participation and presentations at local and regional conferences are further exten-sions of the learning community concept. An excellent example of this idea in action is the community mapping of afterschool programs done in the United Kingdom (see Fordham, 2004). Once committed to the efficacy of quality afterschool programming for positive youth devel-opment, the U. K. government commissioned a nationwide mapping study of afterschool programs, which took 2 years to complete. The baseline data provided by this mapping report became the foundation of resource planning and program quality improvements across the United Kingdom.

In the United States, local communities have begun organizing col-laborative advocacy groups whose informal networking can form the common ground necessary to promote resources, funds, and program improvements. Conference participation and publications can provide momentum for advocating broader programming policies on commu-nity, regional, and national levels. Private foundations such as the C. S. Mott Foundation have supported statewide advocacy efforts to orga-nize and garner resources for local communities wanting to start after-school programs. Through such community activism, civic engagement, research outcomes, and dissemination efforts, the capacity for bridg-ing the achievement gap of minority youth is increased exponentially. Universities begin to more effectively expand their public vision of de-veloping knowledge in the service of society.

Lessons Learned

- Community youth benefit from academic and social modeling provided by university tutors; it is a special relationship for both students and tutors.
- Community youth benefit from enrichment activities provided by university tutors, such as creative writing, arts, science, and physical recreation.

- Classroom teachers and principals benefit from the academic support that students receive from their tutors.
- Classroom teachers benefit from the positive mentoring relationships of tutors and students. Work habits, attitudes, and social skills are improved by this positive mentoring.
- Community partners are actively engaged in teaching university students hands-on strategies for their work with community children.
- Community partners become active, engaged partners with university projects and reciprocal learners with faculty and staff.
- University faculty learn more effective strategies for working with community partners as their ideas are put to the test in community settings.
- Faculty engage with community partners and devise pragmatic solutions with their community partners and students.

CHAPTER 4

Who Owns the Data?
Building a Culture of Evaluation
in Community Settings

> By pursuing an evaluative learning approach, non-profits and funders together as part of a learning community can figure out how to strengthen programs, allocate resources better and share successful models. This makes evaluation work for everyone.
>
> York, "Learning as We Go"

Engaging in evaluation practices that work for everyone creates an ongoing positive evaluation culture, strengthens university and community partnerships, and increases the capacity-building of CBOs in the longer term. Evaluative learning processes can take more time to design and manage initially, which can be frustrating to funders wanting accountability and outcome data quickly. Also, the primary purpose of such processes is to provide internal program evaluation data to allow for the necessary correction and modifications to ensure more positive outcomes for program participants. This necessitates a formative evaluation process model, such as a logic model or an outcomes framework, that is less sophisticated and rigorous in its evaluation design structure but more programmatically useful. Finally, a wide range of differentiated data is collected that has objective components, but which tends to be more subjective overall. Developing evaluation practices that can work in community-based settings is an excellent opportunity to form university–community partnerships, with potential mutual benefit for collaborating partners.

In an afterschool program setting, examples of objective data are demographics, attendance, grade-point average, testing scores, and participant survey information. Subjective data, which enrich and provide a more complex picture of afterschool program data, include site observations, meeting minutes, interviews, and focus group information (Bouffard, 2003), as well as student work samples, tutor reflection logs, course papers, and research projects. The specific details provided by the combination of objective and subjective data support the problem-solving and internal supports that are necessary for sustained and successful afterschool programs.

In their recent research brief on out-of-school time evaluation, Little, Wimer, and Weiss (2008) note that there now exists a growing database of afterschool program evaluations. These evaluations provide increased knowledge about best practices in the field of out-of-school time programming. Over 10 years of research and studies have resulted in the growing consensus that students participating in afterschool programs reap positive benefits academically, socially, and in overall wellness areas.

Flagship evaluations of large-scale afterschool programming have utilized meta-analysis and experimental design evaluation practices to demonstrate positive outcomes. Evaluations of The After School Corporation programs in New York City found that afterschool participants outperformed nonparticipants on math test scores, the New York Regents exams, school attendance rates, and high school credit accrual (Reisner, White, Brimingham, & Welsh, 2001). Similarly, evaluations of Citizen Schools New York demonstrated that participants outperformed nonparticipants on measures such as school attendance, grade promotion, grade and test score measures, and reduced suspension rates (Fabiano, Pearson, Resiner, & Williams, 2006). Findings for Los Angeles's Best After School program, serving over 19,000 students, confirm these positive results. Program participants reported improved school attendance, lower dropout rates, and higher postsecondary aspirations (Huang et al., 2007). Finally, a study of over 200 afterschool programs serving 3,000 low-income, ethnically diverse students from elementary and middle schools around the nation confirmed positive outcomes for afterschool participants (Vandell, Reisner, & Pierce, 2007). This study found significant improvement in student math scores, improved work habits, and reductions in misconduct for both elementary and middle-school students.

The rapid growth and expansion of afterschool programs will continue to require evaluation strategies that provide "good enough" validation of promising practices. Weiss (2005, p. 13) notes that "the characteristics that make after school valuable for youth—flexibility, individualization, and variety of activities—also make evaluation challenging." However, evaluation is necessary to secure adequate funding and resources to sustain afterschool programs and to enable them to provide the structure and guidelines for consistent program quality improvement, as well as to provide baseline data for policymakers seeking to support quality, comprehensive afterschool programs.

While yielding practical results, a formative evaluative model does not provide the sort of design rigor achieved in experimental design models. However, accountability and evaluation design rigor can place inappropriate pressure on practitioners and researchers alike as they attempt to work with community partners in developing program models that promote positive youth outcomes. Given the current consensus that quality afterschool programs can provide valuable academic and social skills support, particularly to low-income minority youth, there are serious ethical concerns to be raised by the control group process required by experimental design models (Bouffard, 2003). At what point should scarce funding resources be given for the development and sustenance of quality afterschool program models serving a great number of children rather than to evaluation processes that result in withholding services to a great number of children? For community-based researchers working with logic models or other evaluative learning models, it is important to acknowledge the limits of what can be claimed from these types of program documentation. Acknowledging that there is much to be gained from continued professional collaboration that keeps a balanced perspective toward developing program needs, evaluative practices, and valid research is but one of the challenges and opportunities for this growing field.

In York's (2003) article for funders and non-profit organizations, he presents an evaluative learning continuum that promotes collaborative work between stakeholders, creates an evaluation environment where all stakeholders are active participants, and creates rich data sources that are fundamental to building successful programs. York raises a number of key questions for program evaluators:

- What is the purpose of the evaluation, and who will be the audience for the findings?
- Who will conduct the evaluation, and who will determine the evaluation questions and design?
- What data are available to address evaluation questions?
- What types of reports, presentations, or data are provided?
- Who will provide interpretive feedback of the findings?
- How frequently will evaluations occur?

In this chapter, the implementation of an evaluation learning model will be discussed, providing both the theory and practical strategies that may be implemented to create an active culture of evaluation that benefits all engaged partners.

Depending on the level of evaluation expertise by the stakeholders, an external evaluator can be supportive in helping to design an evaluation model that "demonstrates relationships between short- and long-term outcomes, program strategies or activities and their outputs, and program inputs or resources (York, 2003). Early in its first year, Project HOPE worked with external evaluators to develop a logic model with short-term, mid-term, and long-term goals. The complete logic model is provided in Appendix C. Once the model has been constructed, the external evaluator's role can shift to one that is integrated into the ongoing evaluative process, providing technical assistance and periodic data review and a type of coaching that keeps the process moving in a focused manner. The community and project staff become primary data collectors of the afterschool program.

Conducting community-based research in minority communities requires respectful consideration of the evaluation purpose and process. This is particularly true when the research involves subjects from vulnerable populations such as school-age children. In addition to respectful consideration of ethical data management, significant consideration needs to be given to research issues such as:

1. How does the research directly benefit afterschool participants and community members?
2. Are the benefits significant enough to be worth the effort of program participants and resource-stretched community staff members?
3. Does the research further contribute to the resources and capacity-building of the CBO?
4. Who learns from the research?

Given the many demands of the under-resourced world of most afterschool programs, research staff need to have the flexibility and capacity to work within the constraints of the community-based research setting. It is not a lab, where the conditions of research can be rigidly constructed and observed. Rather it is a highly interactive, dynamic setting, which demands flexibility and an appreciation of its complexity and social richness (Hirsch, 2005; Theokas, Lerner, Phelps, & Lerner, 2006).

Given these considerations, constraints, and rich opportunities, it is vitally important to work with research methodologies that are compatible with community-based settings. Engagement in community-based settings requires that the initial contact between the researcher and community partner be a productive discussion that results in positive conclusions that the research will be of significant benefit to participants and community members, will be respectful, and will not intrude upon daily program activities.

Constructing a culture of evaluation that will sustain itself and develop productively over the life of a project requires working *with* community partners throughout the evaluation process and having the flexibility to change evaluation practices when indicated by the evaluation process feedback. Typically, this type of evaluation lends itself more readily to qualitative research methodologies that use surveys, observation, interviews, focus group techniques for data collection, and program documentation. However, whether using quantitative or qualitative methodologies, there are basic steps which can be followed in structuring the evaluation process:

1. Define the purpose of the evaluation process to the mutual benefit of all participating partners.
2. Construct data collection and program documentation that can be managed within the community and university partner constraints.
3. Develop formats and feedback loops which regularly share evaluation data with community partners.

DEFINE AN EVALUATION FRAMEWORK THAT MUTUALLY BENEFITS PARTICIPATING PARTNERS

Defining the evaluation's purpose provides an opportunity to begin communication about evaluation in a way that opens and clarifies the evaluation process. This is particularly important in communities where there is residual negative feelings about research, either from past personal experience or from community perceptions. Initially, Project HOPE community partners told university researchers that they would not allow their children to be used as "lab rats" and that they were reluctant to complete surveys, provide demographic information, and sign permission forms. Engaging partners directly in developing project evaluations was only the first step in building an evaluation culture.

For most community partner staff, data collection and program documentation were tedious, time-consuming processes. Their primary concern was providing direct services to afterschool participants and managing the daily operations of their afterschool programs. Data collection, while necessary for long-term program sustainability, was just not a pressing priority given the stress of daily circumstances. However, it was a priority for researchers needing information about program functioning and was necessary for CBOs to prove the effectiveness of their efforts to potential funders and community policymakers. Given these pressures, university project staff had excellent reasons to work closely with community partners in developing data collection procedures that could be maintained and integrated into operational program procedures.

The first and most important step was to work with community partners to develop data collection practices that were acceptable to them and to the university project staff, which needed consistent data input. In the first year of Project HOPE, each of the sites had their own enrollment forms with somewhat different data collected at each site. For project staff, a high priority was the acquisition of consistent demographic and enrollment information across all sites. For community partners, the major concern was preserving their sites' unique identities and continuing to use the forms they had already developed. Also, the partners considered some of the information requested by university staff to be intrusive and not necessary for the functioning of the program.

The solution required a multi-step process. The first step involved collecting the enrollment forms from each site. Using this information, university staff drafted a sample basic enrollment form and a parent permission letter. The form was presented and discussed in subsequent partner meetings where questions were answered about what data were necessary and why. Once the partners contributed their feedback, a final form was developed. The form and permission letter also had to pass the Institutional Review Board approval process at Duke University. Although this process was time consuming, it resulted in an enrollment form and permission letter that have been used in subsequent years with minimal alterations by participating sites. The information from the form then was collected and processed by the university project staff. Once the data collection was complete, it was shared with the afterschool site coordinators during the program year. The data are collected, used, and owned by all participating partners.

Community center staff also underwent necessary differentiated training on the practicalities of getting enrollment information completed and making attendance collection a regular part of the daily program routine. Some of the community center coordinators found it useful to have a group orientation session with entering parents that included information on completing enrollment data forms. Other coordinators held individual parent meetings which included lessons on filling out the enrollment forms and interviews with the parents and students. Both methods gave the center staff an opportunity to go over basic center operations, behavioral expectations, and medical information and to review upcoming activities and events. Attendance information was gathered from student sign-in and sign-out sheets and was used to identify and work with those students who needed help learning how to keep to their established schedules. This elicited reinforcing behaviors such as a daily hello and check-in with a staff member that get the afterschool session off to a good start. The excellent average program attendance rate (92% and 91%, respectively, for the last 2 years) is a testament to the success of this data collection process. University staff working with afterschool staff initially needed to monitor and reinforce regular data documentation using practices that regularly checked that the data collection was occurring. This required training and necessary reinforcement until the task became a routine part of daily practice. Program coordinators often helped each other out as well, with suggestions for what they were doing to create positive attendance performance at their sites. This created a reinforcing culture that supported evaluation goals.

CONSTRUCT DATA COLLECTION AND PROGRAM DOCUMENTATION THAT CAN BE MANAGED WITHIN UNIVERSITY AND COMMUNITY PARTNER CONSTRAINTS

A mistake in the early evaluation process that put pressure on project participants was treating all data collection as equally important. Designing an evaluation framework that is fluid and manageable throughout project engagement requires clarity about what data are necessary for reporting purposes and what data are informative and good to have but less necessary. For example, with afterschool and other school-support programming, necessary quantitative data were demographic data retrieved from enrollment forms and information on program attendance. Other quantitative data of importance were report card grades, testing scores, and grade promotion information. While the latter information was very useful for supporting individual student progress and program evaluation effectiveness, it was also difficult to collect and dependent on local community circumstances. Afterschool program staff routinely cited difficulty collecting student progress information from school settings. Project HOPE experienced the difficulty of having students attend 37 different schools. University project staff proved critical in establishing connections with public schools to allow for a more consistent flow of student information. Afterschool coordinators valued the information gained from regular report card collection and became efficient partners in the report card collection process. They now require participants to bring in their report cards throughout the school year.

Depending on the nature of the research being collected, other types of data collection and program documentation can be more flexibly gathered. Student satisfaction surveys had varying response rates that improved as staff developed more efficient surveying techniques. This required employing different survey techniques until site and university staff worked out a method that worked well for the partnership. For example, while reporting on the activities and events conducted at the afterschool programs was done regularly, it proved not to be necessary for every activity, event, or guest speaker to be documented. Similarly, while student work samples, journals, and activity products are a rich source of documentation, it became evident that sampling was sufficient for documentation purposes. As programs became stabilized and center staff more experienced evaluation participants, program documentation practices were improved, and they became more sophisticated. Researchers working with afterschool programs could also become more discerning about what was necessary and what was not, allowing for a streamlining of the data collection process. Formative evaluation processes that have flexibility in adjusting data collection and documentation procedures are useful for internal evaluation processes. Project HOPE university project staff met regularly with external evaluators to review the logic model, data collection, and conditions in the afterschool programs. These discussions informed data collection procedures and kept them useful to community partners and university staff. Along with joint ownership of the data, data were evaluated and used by all participating partners to promote internal program improvement and increase the sharing of strategies among the afterschool program coordinators. An example of this feedback loop was the regular surveying of afterschool program participants.

Afterschool program participants were surveyed at the beginning and end of the school year. The surveys were administered by university project staff with the assistance of the afterschool program staff. All students were surveyed, with different surveys used for the students in grades K–5 and grades 6–12. The surveys were then compiled into a survey summary that was shared with all of the afterschool site coordinators. Once compiled and shared, the data were used for the multiple purposes of program improvement, reporting to internal and external funders, and project model dissemination. Table 4.1 is an example of the elementary survey that were given at the end of the school year. The data from that survey were compiled so that it could easily be used by afterschool programs and university project staff.

DEVELOP USEFUL DATA-SHARING FORMATS AND FEEDBACK LOOPS

A critical step in constructing a successful culture of evaluation is creating formats and feedback loops which provide community partners with information they can use in a timely manner. University and community partners share a common need for dependable data that can be used for multiple purposes. Internal program evaluation and external reporting to advisory boards, funding sources, and community policymakers are the most common uses of program data. An important first step was to develop interim reporting schema that supported internal program adjustments rather than waiting until the year's end to compile summative data. This may involve a monthly attendance format, enrollment monitoring, quarterly report card summaries, or teacher feedback on student progress. Tutors provided weekly process notes that were read by center coordinators and university staff and used for determining necessary strategic adjustments to ensure students' academic progress. Getting information to coordinators also resulted in more transparent and open communication about student progress, program functioning, and necessary trouble-shooting. Ultimately, interim data reporting supported the importance of data collection and program documentation processes, giving a needed encouragement to the overall process. It's an intermediate incentive that sustained the longer term effort.

An example of interim data reporting was the balance card created by HOPE's university project staff (see Table 4.2). The balance card emerged out of the periodic evaluation reviews with external evaluators. It was

TABLE 4.1. Elementary School Survey Responses, Spring 2009

Site 1: 30	Yes (no.)	Yes (%)	No (no.)	No (%)
1. I like coming to the program	26	84%	4	13%
2. I feel comfortable talking to the staff.	25	81%	5	16%
3. I can get help with my work.	27	87%	2	6%
4. I am doing better in school	27	87%	3	10%
Site 2: 6	Yes #	Yes %	No #	No %
1. I like coming to the program	6	100%	0	0%
2. I feel comfortable talking to the staff.	5	83%	1	17%
3. I can get help with my work.	6	100%	0	0%
4. I am doing better in school.	6	100%	0	0%
Site 3: 34	Yes #	Yes %	No #	No %
1. I like coming to the program.	33	97%	1	3%
2. I feel comfortable talking to the staff.	30	88%	4	12%
3. I can get help with my homework.	33	97%	1	3%
4. I am doing better in school.	33	97%	1	3%
Site 4: 17	Yes #	Yes %	No #	No %
1. I like coming to the program.	16	94%	1	6%
2. I feel comfortable talking to the staff.	12	71%	4	24%
3. I can get help with my homework.	16	100%	0	0%
4. I am doing better in school.	15	88%	1	6%
Site 5: 3	Yes #	Yes %	No #	No %
1. I like coming to the program.	1	33%	2	67%
2. I feel comfortable talking to the staff.	3	100%	0	0%
3. I can get help with my homework.	3	100%	0	0%
4. I am doing better in school.	1	33%	2	66%%
Site 6: 17	Yes #	Yes %	No #	No %
1. I like coming to the program.	16	94%	1	6%
2. I feel comfortable talking to program staff.	15	88%	2	12%
3. I can get help with my work.	17	100%	0	0%
4. I am doing better in school.	16	94%	1	6%
TOTAL:108	Yes #	Yes %	No #	No %
1. I like coming to the program.	98	91%	9	8%
2. I feel comfortable talking to staff.	90	83%	15	14%
3. I can get help with my work.	102	94%	3	3%
4. I am doing better in school.	98	91%	5	5%

TABLE 4.2. Balance Card, 2008–2009

	Site 1 (elementary)	Site 1 (secondary)	Site 2	Site 3	Site 4	Site 5 (elementary)	Site 5 (secondary)	Site 6
Weekly Open Hours	6	3	20	16	20	20	20	20
Fall Student Enrollment	10	4	27	4	62	17	4	67
Spring Student Enrollment	10	4	30	6	59	17	5	73
Student Return Rate 07/08–08/09	64%	100%	67%	25%	48%	59%	75%	70%
Mid-Year Student Retention	100%	100%	100%	100%	94%	94%	100%	97%
End-of-Year Student Retention	100%	100%	100%	100%	95%	100%	100%	94%
Fall Student Attendance	96%	83%	83%	93%	94%	98%	100%	95%
Spring Student Attendance	88%	96%	81%	91%	93%	95%	91%	94%
08-09 Student Attendance	91%	90%	82%	92%	94%	96%	95%	94%
08-09 All Sites Attendance: 92%								
Report Card Return Rate (1st)	80%	100%	67%	100%	100%	65%	100%	97%
Report Card Return Rate (2nd)	100%	100%	87%	100%	100%	100%	100%	96%
Report Card Return Rate (3rd)	100%	100%	90%	100%	95%	100%	80%	95%
Students w/ C Average or Higher (1st)	80%	75%	56%	75%	92%	65%	50%	91%
Students w/ C Average or Higher (2nd)	100%	75%	83%	75%	98%	94%	40%	94%
Students w/ C Average or Higher (3rd)	100%	50%	83%	83%	93%	94%	20%	91%
Students w/ C Average or Higher Final Grade	100%	75%	83%	83%	91%	100%	40%	95%
08-09 All Students with C Average or Higher: 91%								
Students w/ B Average or Higher (1st)	50%	50%	48%	0%	25%	41%	25%	78%
Students w/ B Average or Higher (2nd)	80%	50%	60%	50%	77%	70%	20%	75%
Students w/ B Average or Higher (3rd)	80%	25%	77%	60%	84%	76%	0%	78%
Students w/ B Average or Higher Final Grade	70%	50%	70%	33%	83%	76%	0%	84%
08-09 All Students with B Average or Higher: 76%								

quickly obvious that waiting for final, summative data simply took too long to be useful in evaluating student progress and program impacts. This was brought home in the first year when staff didn't find out until May that one student was failing virtually all subjects and wouldn't pass his grade. This outcome was unacceptable. The purpose of the balance card was to create a format that could be updated twice in a program year (January and July). It would define common program elements and provide a minimal basis for program comparisons. This format became a rough yardstick for program coordinators, university project staff, and administrators to view how the programs were doing individually and in comparison with each other. The information was shared internally and became the basis for many productive program improvement discussions.

Recognition and resolution of significant tension points early in the evaluation supported the growth of a positive evaluation culture. Two important elements have already been discussed: (1) agreeing collectively on project goals and objectives, and (2) establishing reasonable routines for data collection that support project documentation and reporting requirements.

Other potential tension points may also emerge that are common to the evaluation process, including student privacy issues, ownership of the data, and any existing residual issues from having had poor evaluation experiences in the past. Recognizing and carefully managing each of these issues can help make the evaluation process mutually beneficial for all partners.

Data Access and Privacy Issues

Formal aspects of the evaluation process can also strengthen the evaluation culture if managed carefully. Universities have the advantage of structured Institutional Review Board requirements, which can be stringent for projects working with vulnerable populations. This is usually a negotiated process and, when handled well, can reinforce ethical reporting practices that are respectful of individual, family, and community privacy. Human subjects research privacy limitations require that project leaders gain parental and subject permission and explain the research process throughout the project's data collection stages. Collecting vital demographic information requires thoughtful negotiation and alternative methods for parents to follow. For example, parents may hesitate to give afterschool personnel access to school records or teacher contact. School personnel, also, may be reluctant to share student progress of behavioral information with afterschool personnel, even with written parental permission. This reluctance can be overcome as relationships are built with consistent, trustworthy communication from project and afterschool program staff. A further reinforcing structure is when the permission-gathering and data-collection formats are repeatedly used and become a routine component of program practice. The sometimes frightening language of evaluation (e.g., "research investigation," "documentation," and "research subject") is eased as experience with the process is no longer perceived as dangerous. Sample parent permission letters and enrollment forms are provided in Appendices A and B.

Data Ownership and Use

Another sensitive evaluation consideration is responding to the issue of who owns the data and how the data will be used. After the data are collected, the most frequent complaint from community partners working with university personnel is that either the data are never reported back to them, or the data come back so much later that they are no longer useful. A further concern is that, since it is data about their community, they should have access to it in a format that the CBO can use for their own program evaluation, reporting, and fund-raising efforts. The creation of the feedback loop, with information being shared and discussed at predictable intervals, reinforces the value of the data collection and program documentation efforts. Partners will then become enthusiastic data-consumers and much more willing to work toward the common goal of getting good and useful information.

A related evaluation consideration is to realistically assure that there are personnel who have dedicated time to the evaluation process. Trained university staff who are skilled at working in multiple community contexts are able to work closely with community partners, particularly in the early stages of the evaluation process. As the project grows and its research dimensions increase, it may be important to add additional support staff or to further differentiate roles and responsibilities so the work can continue without overburdening individual project staff or CBOs. University students who are well-supervised by project staff or faculty can actively participate in the project monitoring and evaluation process. However, each individual handling student and program data needs to be aware that they are entering a partnership where privacy and trust are valued components of the process.

LEARNING FROM THE EVALUATION PROCESS

As the basic evaluation processes are underway and producing outcome and program documentation data, external evaluators can revise the collaborative partner role and begin to deepen the data-collection process. This is where their insider/outsider observer status can be critical to program improvements. The external evaluator can meet with the project staff regularly to review outcome data and the data-gathering process. In their coaching role, they can work with project staff to determine what data are worth collecting, what documentation formats need to be revised, how revisions may improve efficiency, and what adjustments are necessary to improve the data being collected. One example of this emerged immediately in Project HOPE when the staff was highly dissatisfied with the initial student surveys for secondary students that were used in Year 1 and Year 2. The external evaluators researched other secondary survey models and worked with project staff to develop a survey that was easy to administer and would produce differentiated data from the secondary student participants. As an example of the evaluative learning process, it wasn't until Year 3 that surveys were designed that worked for the majority of participants, and not until Years 4 and 5 that a survey collection process was developed that yielded a significantly higher percentage of survey completions from student participants. We had to continually return back to the drawing board until a workable format and process was developed.

A further positive aspect of the external evaluator can be the development of their role into that of an outsider observer. This function can be performed through periodic site observations and meeting attendance, which forms the basis for quarterly or year-end reports. Further program observations can be gathered by outside evaluators through interviews and focus groups conducted with other participants who have an opportunity to be engaged with the afterschool program. This may be parents, community partners working with the afterschool programs, university faculty, or student staff participants. This type of data collection further expands the "outside eyes" component, giving program staff a way to take stock of how others are viewing program development. As an integrated part of the evaluation learning process, which occurs on a periodic basis, project staff have data they can use to further improve their programs. The information gathered from these additional documentation processes is shared with all project participants, using reporting language and formats that can be readily understood by all. The reports can be discussed individually with community partners and as a group to promote problem solving and the sharing of successful program management strategies. The predictable routine of this process can create a collaborative atmosphere with the external evaluators, overcoming suspicions and barriers. In this manner, a freer exchange of constructive feedback reinforces the evaluation learning process. Project HOPE staff became comfortable with evaluation of the feedback from the external evaluators, and this made it easier to absorb critical feedback into program improvement. In one significant incident, the afterschool program coordinators insisted that the external evaluator share critical feedback in an open meeting that included a major funding project officer. This was a watershed moment, proving that evaluation was useful and valued by the community partners and that the external evaluators offered critical feedback that would improve their programs.

A parent focus group conducted by the external evaluators in May 2007 provides another example of this effective process (Upton & Whittington, 2007). Parent responses to external evaluators provided afterschool site coordinators and university project staff with positive and critical feedback that helped improve parent interactions and support. Positive feedback was unanimous that the afterschool programs were doing well in a range of areas, including reading, math, and writing (Upton & Whittington, 2007, p. 2):

> My daughter's reading has really (been)helped since she has been coming to the center.

> My daughter has been focusing more on math.

> My son's writing has improved.

In addition, parents praised the enrichment and social skills activities, with special note made of the health component of the program.

> I like the part where the lady comes from the health department. She comes in with the preteens and really teaches them about the development of themselves, the different kinds of STDs. You have to have a parental consent for them to teach them, but it teaches them as preteens about what's really out there and what's going on and the kids seem to open up to her, whereas they probably wouldn't open up with a parent.

Parents also noted that the afterschool program site coordinator would communicate frequently with them about their student's progress or challenges that the student might be facing. The site coordinators also provided information about school issues and community resources (p. 8):

> I get the information. She will call on the phone. I know way ahead of time if something is going on (at the center). They send letters home with the kids. And if she doesn't come, the director will call you.

> She will call parents. She will go to the house and knock on your door.

> If your child is having an issue (at the center), you better believe that she will let you know! If she doesn't talk to you on the phone, she will come by your house on her way home.

Parents made significant suggestions for afterschool improvements. They wanted increased services made available to a wider age range of students. Their recommendations included

- extending the program hours;
- increased time with tutors;
- activities that would be attractive to older students;
- enrichment activities across all the sites (some sites had more or better activities).

The external evaluator focused on strategies for the afterschool programs to improve services to parents. They recommended

- more tools and guidance that they could use to reinforce their children's progress at home;
- parent workshops that would review grade level skills development and test-taking strategies;
- involving parents in suggestions for program improvements.

In addition to the external evaluators, university undergraduate participation in the evaluation process provided another useful and unique lens on program development. University undergraduates are an imaginative source of energy, enthusiasm, and creative thinking that can positively impact afterschool programs. Given appropriate training and supervision, they can provide vital academic support and mentoring components to afterschool programs. Their critical and analytic faculties can also assist in the evaluation and program development process. During the tutoring process, tutors can be required to keep reflection logs that detail their work with afterschool program students. These logs can provide lesson planning details, raise issues that need to be addressed by program staff, and also reflect on the overall progress of the program. They provide immediate feedback and a prompt review, and are an excellent evaluative source of program functioning. Because they are a written record, they can also become an additional ongoing program documentation source. End-of-semester university student surveys provide critical feedback to project administrators about what went well and what tutoring aspects still need work.

Through internships and community-based research projects, undergraduates can provide an additional evaluation and research function. This is an area that needs to be carefully developed and supervised.

Enthusiastic university students can often demand valuable afterschool program staff time to conduct interviews or meet documentation or resource needs. Coordinator accessibility needs to be respected, and university students should be helped to understand the reciprocal nature of the research process. Through time, resources, and direct service delivery, undergraduates need to give at least as good as they are getting from the afterschool program staff. When managed well, valuable products can emerge from this process. University undergraduates can develop activities and mentoring groups that directly benefit afterschool program students. An example was the research work done by the Duke–Durham Scholars with the summer learning camps of the community partners. These undergraduates completed summer internships and a fall research course that resulted in projects useful to the community partners organizations. One project curriculum on health and nutrition developed by a Duke–Durham Scholar is still used, several years later, by the Camp Calvary summer camp program. Finally, undergraduates can examine their own processes. This may involve closely examining the tutor–tutee relationship or looking at the actual tutor training necessary to address the cultural competency issues that confront the novice tutor. Students, with their infinite capacity for questioning and their desire to make things better, can become excellent resources for contributing to the evaluation learning process.

OWNING AND USING THE DATA

Data collected through the evaluation learning process becomes collectively owned and used by the active participants engaged in the program documentation process. Enrollment, attendance, report card, grade-point average, and testing score data can be collected and worked into a streamlined, usable format that is useful to afterschool program staff, university project staff, tutors and volunteers, and external evaluators. Consistent access to these data on an interim basis is a significant boost to the academic and social skills support that is provided to struggling students. Once school system personnel become familiar with the realistic assistance afterschool program staff and tutors offer their students, they usually are more willing to share information and strategies that they feel will be helpful to the students. Similarly, parents can also be assisted in working on specific strategies that will be helpful to their students. Table 4.3 gives examples of results from the teacher survey data

TABLE 4.3. Teacher Survey Data 2009

Dev Area (60)	Needs Improvement	Maintain	Improve	Maintain or Improve (no.)	Maintain or Improve (%.)	Improve (%)
Reading	14	20	25	45	75%	42%
Math	13	15	32	47	78%	53%
Organizational Skills	14	25	19	44	73%	32%
Homework On Time	6	25	29	54	90%	48%
Homework Accuracy	5	23	30	53	88%	50%
70% Quiz	7	31	18	49	82%	30%
Class Behavioral Skills						
Class Participation	7	27	26	53	88%	43%
Attentive in Class	9	27	24	51	85%	40%
Completes Classwork	7	28	18	46	77%	30%
Study Skills	15	28	14	42	70%	23%
Overall Academic Performance	11	18	31	49	82%	52%

and highlights the productive exchange of information that can result from this process. It should be noted that the project staff struggled for several years to get teachers to respond to the afterschool surveys and rarely had more than a dozen or so replies. After careful nurturing by the liaison coordinator, the numbers increased every year to the current level of 50–60 teachers responding every year.

Sharing database information and survey and observation reporting creates a more transparent operating environment, and this in turn builds trust and engenders more positive working relationships. Through the repetition of the data collection and feedback loop cycle, community and university partners are able to build collective ownership and use of the database. This allows for multiple uses of the information and broader dissemination of the project model.

Evaluation information can be used internally and externally to improve program functioning, provide accountability to existing and future funders, and disseminate information about the project model. Internal documentation uses include monitoring individual student progress, assisting tutors in developing successful academic support strategies, and monitoring program management practices. Once this information is collected and analyzed into its summative formats, the data become usable for community partners to do their own grant writing, fund-raising, and internal reporting for their boards or other community agencies.

Development of lessons learned, collaborative models, and evaluation research can then become useful to broader audiences. The data gathered from Project HOPE research have been shared with local, regional, and national audiences. Locally, the research has been a significant component of advocacy efforts for improved afterschool and summer learning programs for low-income minority youth. Regional and national presentations and workshops have addressed afterschool program development, the role of undergraduate service learning in supporting student achievement, and building evaluative cultures in community-based settings. In addition, program products such as tutor orientation instructional materials, training manuals, and program curriculum have been useful products of the program model development.

SUMMARY

The scarcity of systematic information collected and analyzed on the productive operation of afterschool programs requires the attention of evaluators willing to develop research models that can be realistically managed in the underresourced afterschool program environment. Collaborative partnership with university partners is a viable model that is able to provide the combination of structure and flexibility needed to attract and sustain a variety of funding sources. University students, staff, and faculty are renewable, available resources to many communities. With their resources organized effectively into service learning and evaluation learning structures, university and community partners can form effective, sustainable partnerships.

The final evaluation report from the external evaluators on Project HOPE was completed in October 2007. The report noted that Project HOPE had accomplished positive university and community impacts in several areas, particularly with afterschool program students, program sustainability and infrastructure, and institutional service-learning development. Afterschool student impacts included:

- student academic growth on report cards and end-of-grade reading scores;
- student, parent, and teacher surveys indicating numerous benefits;
- increased program stability as indicated by site staff retention, student attendance, and retention rates;
- increased number of Duke tutors who contributed a high number of hours to the afterschool program; and
- enrichment activities that complemented academic support.

Sustainability impacts were demonstrated in additional funding, program infrastructure development, communication, and staff stability. These include:

- continued multiple funding sources for programming;
- university administration support for funding;
- establishment of strong underlying infrastructure and collaborative relationships with partners; and
- stability of staff across all levels contributing to project consistency.

Service-learning development was particularly noted in the final report:

- Service learning became an institutionalized and an integral part of Duke undergraduate education.
- The involvement of Duke students in afterschool programming through service-learning courses became an important component in engaging a growing number of students in Durham communities.
- University students who worked with HOPE programs mentioned the impact on their students and also the long-term impacts on their own lives:

   It impacted me academically in that I now recognize that knowledge comes from many different sources, not just academic ones. I expanded my horizons.

   Project HOPE is a great experience that reminded me why I chose the profession of teaching—it solidified that choice. It also reinforced my decision to teach in a low-income school rather than a private school. It was not a one-way street—I learned from them. What do they think about Duke? I became more aware of the perceptions of the community as to Duke's place in the Durham community. (Upton & Whittington, 2007, p. 7)

- HOPE staff and participating students and faculty expanded their knowledge beyond their academic discipline area and learned from community partners.
- HOPE contributed to a working partnership between Duke University and North Carolina Central University.

The report also commented on the challenges facing Project HOPE:

- Some of the afterschool programs would benefit from increased emphasis on academic quality.
- Parent feedback suggests that the parents of older students would be more likely to be involved if there were more opportunities for

them to participate as partners rather than just as a recipient of services.

- Site coordinators should be encouraged to share the lessons they have learned.
- Reviews and evaluations of the products prepared by the Duke–Durham Scholars can be used more effectively.
- Implementation of strategies for recruiting and managing an increased number of tutors can be improved.
- Tutors would benefit from additional preliminary information about the project and their roles.
- Consideration needs to be given to the development of programs specifically designed to meet the needs of secondary students.

Developing university and community partnerships that combine learning and evaluative practices that are reflective, renewable resources can be mutually beneficial to all partnership participants. The sustained development of the afterschool programs has had a lasting impact on its students, with the site coordinators now able to claim recent high school, college, and professional school graduates. University staff has equally proud Duke graduates pursuing professional careers and activities that take the lessons learned to new ventures, communities, and social policy impacts. Faculty continues to be challenged to revise courses and develop working models and research strategies that spread the knowledge gained to broader contexts.

The synergy created by the university and community partnership has had positive impacts for all participants. The ripple effects continue to be experienced by those who have been involved in the university and community partnership from the beginning as well as by those who have joined over time. Significant challenges remain and will need to be confronted as partners face the next decade.

Lessons Learned

- Evaluation is a learning process that needs to be reciprocal with collaborative partners.
- Collaborative partners need to be involved in determining what data are useful and should be collected.
- Data collection processes and procedures need to be transparent.
- Data collection needs to be a routine part of program administration.

- Training and support throughout the data collection process must involve collaboration between partners.
- Respect for partner priorities must be maintained throughout the data documentation process.
- A positive, regular feedback loop should be created that provides collaborating partners with regular data report updates and analysis.
- A culture of sharing of information, resources, and ideas for program improvement should be established.

CHAPTER 5

Where Have We Been?
Where Are We Going?

In her final year as president of Duke University, Nannerl O. Keohane reflected on her presidential tenure in her Founder's Day address and included the work of the Duke–Durham Neighborhood Partnership in her remarks:

> The Neighborhood Partnership Initiative has been one of the best aspects of our outreach as a university. In a focused and systematic way, we have, together, made some fundamental difference for good in the lives of our neighbors on all sides. In schools and churches, clinics, neighborhood centers, and renovated housing, Duke people are out there everyday working with our neighbors as partners." (Keohane, 2006)

In this final chapter, the results of the first decade of the Duke–Durham Neighborhood Partnership (DDNP) will be reviewed along with the strategic planning and new directions for the next decade of the partnership. These reflections will take us back to the initial questions posed in the first chapter:

- What can community-based afterschool programs do to promote positive youth development with low-income minority youth?
- How do we successfully manage a collaborative university and community partnership with the complex requirements of joint program administration?
- Who learns? What is learned?
- How do we create a culture of evaluation that provides sufficient information for program improvement and meets the needs of funding sources?
- What is necessary to sustain programs? Can our programming be replicated in other communities?

- How does university–community engagement change universities, communities, and student participants?

The DDNP was a major initiative of President Keohane and received her leadership support throughout the 11 years of her administrative tenure. On July 1, 2004, Richard H. Brodhead succeeded Nannerl O. Keohane as president of Duke University, creating an opportunity for self-assessment and review of DDNP strategic goals and priorities. John Burness, in preparation for the transition to the new presidency, initiated strategic planning within the Office of Community Affairs and its work with the DDNP. At this time, it was evident that there was a need to examine the results of the first decade and determine strategic goals for the next decade. Two firms, the Center for Assessment and Policy Development (CAPD) and Marga, Inc., were hired by the Duke Endowment to conduct a broad evaluation of the Office of Community Affairs and the DDNP. The planning for the evaluation was scheduled for the spring of 2006. This would allow community and university partners to take advantage of the end of the academic year, normally an excellent time for reflection and evaluation.

The welcomed spring break ended with significant consequences for the university and the Durham community. While taking a brief vacation in California, I received a series of frantic emails from close friends and family members saying that I must turn on the news. I promptly did and was stunned to get the early reports of what has become known as the Duke lacrosse incident. As we were to learn, on March 13, 2006, members of the Duke lacrosse team held a party at the residence of the team's captains. Two women, one African American and the other of mixed ethnicity, were hired to perform at the party. Shortly after arriving at the party, an argument ensued and the young women left the scene. One of the women was later taken to Duke University medical center, where she was examined and treated. The young woman accused three lacrosse team players of sexual assault. The ensuing media storm disrupted the Duke campus for the remaining weeks of the semester. The lacrosse season was cancelled and the lacrosse coach lost his job. A full year later, on April 11, 2007, North Carolina Attorney General Roy Cooper dropped all charges and declared the three lacrosse players innocent. The lead prosecutor in the case also lost his job and law license. The legal suits and countersuits from this case continue to the present day. Eventually, they will be resolved, books will be written, and the impact of the case will be studied from multiple perspectives.

As the news spread throughout the Durham and Duke University community, the business of coursework, tutoring, and schooling had to continue. Never mind that the roads were clogged with media trucks and it was hard to visit the west campus without stepping over large cables or avoiding the glare of reporting kleig lights. An immediate question that had to be answered was the safety of afterschool students and Duke tutors as they moved from school to campus to home over the remaining weeks of the school year. Tutoring was briefly suspended for a couple of days to allow university project staff and community partners to assess the situation. The decision was made to give tutors the option of completing their tutoring for the remainder of the semester. We were close enough to the semester's end to take this step. However, all participants were keenly aware that the crucial end-of-grade tests were only 3 weeks away, and the tutors were anxious to complete their students' final test preparation. Of the several hundred tutors working in the community, only one tutor quit.

The community partners reassured the Duke students, letting them know that they valued their work and that they were not responsible for the incident. One afterschool site coordinator gave her Duke tutors an example of what it means to be a community leader. In a corner of her concrete playground area, she installed a set of raised garden beds. After planting these with her usual mix of flowers and vegetables for the summer, she put up a large sign over the garden, stating, "Keep Project HOPE alive!" It was exactly the emotional boost that tutors and project staff needed to maintain their composure and commitment to the afterschool students. University project staff were consistently visible during this last month to provide further confidence to tutors and community partners that the program would continue smoothly. The tutoring work continued steadily with the result that the afterschool students scored well on their end-of-grade tests. Students and their Duke tutors learned the importance of remaining positively focused on what matters in the midst of powerful and potentially explosive distractions.

A broader question of significance faced the Office of Community Affairs staff: Should they continue with the evaluation of the DDNP? In addition to the organization challenges of managing a major comprehensive evaluation with two different firms, there was now the added pressure of doing so in the midst of a media vortex like none other in the university's history. The Duke Endowment officers were concerned and said that they would support the decision of the Office of Community Affairs as to whether they would continue the evaluation or postpone it to a later date. The Office of Community Affairs staff discussed their options and decided to proceed with the evaluation. They believed that the work of the DDNP had a strong enough foundation and relationships that were sturdy enough to sustain the questioning and probing of an evaluation process. This trust in the strength of the established relationships was borne out and noted in the CAPD/Marga report (Liederman, Liederman, Maurasse, & James, 2006):

> One indicator of the level of trust that has been established is the degree to which the DDNP's work was not stalled by the lacrosse incident. Additionally, the DDNP community partners did not raise the incident as a priority concern. In situations where relationships are not strong and tensions are high, incidents that appear to be even remotely symbolic of negative relations can explode. Ongoing, healthy relations between a university and community allow collaborative projects and initiatives to progress with fewer disruptions and distractions. The DDNP continues to invest in relationships, and that investment is paying off, in turn, enabling the right environment for the continuation and enhancement of the DDNP's work. (p. 66)

A second report produced in the fall of 2007 by the Rensselaerville Institute was more focused on the specific outcomes of the DDNP's first decade. In addition to the lacrosse incident, university and community relations were discussed and examined in what, at the time, felt like an endless circular loop. Community members were concerned about whether the university would continue its resource commitments. Duke parents and students raised concerns about safety issues. Faculty ambiguity about the role of service and its relationship to the primary mission of the university were openly expressed. The Durham community did what it does best—it faced its problems and continued working on them.

The accomplishments outlined in the two reports focused on the four major areas of the DDNP: academic and youth development, neighborhood stabilization, Duke civic engagement, and strengthening our partners. The latter category, strengthening our partners, appeared to overlap with the other three areas of study and so was dropped as a separate category. The reports noted significant progress in each area along with altered community and university attitudes, reflecting the mutual, beneficial aspects of the university–community partnership.

Although not exhaustive, some of the major accomplishments in each area are reviewed in this chapter, along with discussions of the most important portions of the reports. The full reports are available online at http://community.duke.edu.

ACADEMIC AND YOUTH DEVELOPMENT

The academic and youth development area included Project HOPE afterschool programs; school-based tutoring programs; school-based academic, arts, and other enrichment programs; and community-based mentoring programs. The CAPD/Marga and Rensselaerville Institute reports noted a number of accomplishments:

- Programs have reached all DDNP schools, hundreds of children, and dozens of teachers with a wide range of academic enrichments in literacy, science, cultural, arts, tutoring and mentoring.
- There were numerous individual participant success stories.
- Attention was given to logic models, evaluation, and tracking results.
- Duke students were exposed to urban public school challenges.

Additional accomplishments noted in the reports were:

- program responsiveness to community requests;
- use of best-practice models and high-quality implementation;
- staff commitment;
- tutor training;
- strategies focused on outcomes; and
- support from the Office of Community Affairs.

The reports also noted challenges that needed further work:

- Goals needed to be articulated as measurable benchmarks.
- Neighborhood boundaries were not aligned with census tracts.
- Community-based programming didn't align with DDNP schools.
- The sum of individual gains of students involved in DDNP programs was not enough to improve school test score outcomes.
- Test scores themselves were an erratic source of assessment.
- The high turnover of school leadership was problematic.

Academic and youth development were major priorities of the DDNP, receiving attention and resources from several sources. The Office of Community Affairs differentiated its efforts between school-based programming and community-based afterschool programming. As detailed in prior chapters, the accomplishments of Project HOPE afterschool programs continued to be consistently positive, with each year building upon prior results. By the end of the 2008 academic year, Project HOPE's 1,107 tutors had provided 16,962 tutoring hours in the afterschool programs serving predominantly low-income minority students. Afterschool student grades and test scores defied the odds that their demographics suggested, with results such as a 92% afterschool program attendance rate, 91% of HOPE students sustaining a "C" average, and 76% sustaining a "B" average or above on their report cards. The overall end-of-grade test score averages for the past 7 years were a 69% passing rate in reading and a 64% passing rate in math. For these students, bridging the achievement gap is a daily reality that is being met as they are routinely successful academically and socially in their classrooms.

In addition to the work being done in the afterschool programs, expanding school-based programming also demonstrated evidence of success. Tutoring programs such as Partners for Success, America Reads/America Counts, the freshman orientation program, and Project CHILD provided thousands of hours of individual tutoring in Durham Public Schools. The community affairs staff worked with staff from the Program in Education and the Community Service Center to implement these tutoring programs. Additional academic support was leveraged by the DDNP's schools partnership coordinator, David Stein. One example of Stein's innovative programming was BOOST. Funded by the Howard Hughes Medical Institute, Duke graduate students mentored 5th graders who were transitioning to middle school through highly interactive math and science activities. Stein also leveraged university resources to include an interactive science lab at E.K. Powe Elementary School and outdoor learning environments at two other partner schools. Arts enrichment programs were negotiated through Duke Performances and Duke arts departments. Another program, School Days, offers Duke campus visits each fall to local 8th graders with tours of classrooms, labs, student dorms, and the food court. Community-based youth development programs such as Partners for Youth and Rites of Passage offered mentoring and academic assistance to high school students. Each of these programs supported students in their goals to graduate from high school and attend college or post-secondary school. The combination of all of these programs contains a multitude of positive touches between Duke students, faculty, and project staff with their student participants and community partners. According to the Rensselaerville Institute report:

> As important as are structured programs (such as tutoring or mentoring), students and parents report that the greatest gains have come from the

personal touch of over 500 Duke students who come to neighborhood schools and centers each semester to interact personally with students. These personal relationships [and] the message of optimism and care from young people, who are seen as genuinely wanting to connect to these students' lives, [are] even more powerful at improving lives than is specific help with homework and lessons. We see many ways to build that force much more explicitly in the next decade of the Partnership. (Williams, 2007, p. 2)

NEIGHBORHOOD STABILIZATION

Another key area of impact by the DDNP noted in the two reports was neighborhood stabilization. This strategic planning area involved increasing the availability of affordable housing, improving access to health care, and lowering crime in DDNP neighborhoods. By the time of the two reports in 2006–2007, improvement was noted in all of these areas.

Accomplishments stated by the CAPD/Marga and Rensselaerville Institute reports included

- housing stock investment for new or revitalized homes;
- neighborhood and community center development;
- increased community decision-making on community concerns;
- increased civic engagement by residents;
- increased health services through two neighborhood clinics; and
- student opportunities in neighborhood organizing, integration into the community, and skill development.

Areas that worked well toward this strategic goal were:

- availability of the Office of Community Affairs personnel to coordinate activities;
- credibility added to neighborhood improvement efforts by the Southwest Central Durham Quality of Life Committee; and
- highlighting of community traditions.

Challenges in this area were largely focused on expanding the work currently being done:

- better use of qualitative data to track indicators;
- increased participation by renters, landlords, and others;

- caution that improving neighborhoods may also contribute to changing neighborhood culture;
- the importance of being direct about goals and outcomes; and
- effective Southwest Central Durham (SWCD) neighborhood Quality of Life committee looked to for expansion or replication in other Durham neighborhoods.

The reports noted that 264 houses were built or reconstructed. This included homes in the Crest Street, Trinity Heights, and Southwest Central Durham. Housing development in the Trinity Heights neighborhood converted former crime-laden vacant lots that adjoined Duke's east campus into a thriving neighborhood of Duke faculty and staff-owned homes. This is now a neighborhood of over 40 homes and townhouses that were awarded recognition by the Historic Preservation Society of Durham for designs that worked well with existing neighborhood structures.

The bulk of the renovated and reconstructed homes were built in the Walltown and SWCD neighborhoods. The Self-Help Corporation provided support that was crucial to this affordable housing development, and the Habitat for Humanity and the Durham Land Trust joined in, focusing most of their efforts in SWCD. In SWCD, a vibrant community organizing effort led by the DDNP coordinator, Mayme Webb-Bledsoe, resulted in the successful Quality of Life project. This project has been the driving force for generating community reforms, celebrating community history and traditions, and reviving efforts to recognize the historical value of this vibrant community. Pauli Murray Place, a development of 14 affordable homes in SWCD, honors a major human rights activist, Pauli Murray. Rev. Murray was raised by her family, the Fitzgeralds, in the West End neighborhood and wrote a fascinating memoir, *Proud Shoes,* about her family and experiences growing up in the West End community of Durham. A major community art project, Face-Up, created murals featuring Pauli Murray and other community activists in 8 sites and 14 murals throughout Durham. Since the 2007 report, homes continue to be built and renovated in DDNP neighborhoods. These efforts have led to lower rental home rates and an increased number of owner-occupied homes in the DDNP neighborhoods. Affordable senior housing is also being addressed with the recent opening of a major new senior apartment complex, Maplewood Park, in SWCD. In a lovely intergenerational planning touch, a children's park was completed adjacent to Maplewood Park. Ms. Webb-Bledsoe continues to work on future neighborhood improvement projects in SWCD and has been tapped as a consultant to the city of Durham for her community development expertise.

Crime issues were addressed in the DDNP neighborhoods through local community discussions with Partners Against Crime initiatives. Duke police officers now patrol neighborhoods adjacent to the campus, providing an additional police presence to supplement Durham police efforts. Duke assisted in keeping a police substation in an SWCD neighborhood shopping center. The university also purchased two properties in Walltown and SWCD that were drug havens in these neighborhoods. These properties now provide residences for Duke Chapel interns and a nonprofit organization, adding a positive presence in their respective neighborhoods. Residents of DDNP neighborhoods noted that their communities have increased in value, are more aesthetically pleasing, and are safer (Williams, 2008).

Another contribution to the health of the DDNP neighborhoods was the development of community health clinics. Access to health care had been noted as a critical concern for community residents. Duke's medical center had long been involved in providing medical care to the Durham community. However, community residents stated that they needed health care that was affordable and closer to their communities. Along with its afterschool programming initiatives, Project HOPE funding included start-up funding resources for community-based clinics. Working with Susan Yaggy and her Division of Community Medicine team, two community-based health care clinics were established in Walltown and SWCD. Both of these clinics have been highly successful. The clinic in the Community Family Life Center at Lyon Park in SWCD needed to expand both its facilities and its hours within 6 months of its opening. Wellness clinics were also opened in two DDNP schools, George Watts Elementary School and the E. K. Powe Elementary School. Based on these successful models, three other clinics were opened at Glenn School, Southern High School, and the recently opened Holton Recreation Center. The wellness clinics were a good example of how the university–community partnership generated a community-based concept, collaborated on funding, and piloted small experimental models. Like the afterschool programs, once the programs were productive and popular with the community, they become models for other collaborative agencies and were expanded to additional sites.

An important note needs to be made about the role of recreation centers in community life. As Michael Palmer states regularly when giving DDNP tours, community centers have the capacity to function as "human service" malls. Instead of a shopping mall, the community center functions as a hub for a variety of social service needs in a concept similar to the settlement houses of an earlier urban America. The DDNP was intensely involved in the negotiations involving the development of the Community Family Life Center at Lyon Park. Lyon Park, an abandoned former African American elementary school, was an eyesore of historic dimensions in the West End community. Initial advocacy for the reconstruction of Lyon Park Elementary School into a community recreation center was begun by the neighborhood Reunions Committee. These efforts were continued by the nonprofit organization, Calvary Ministries of the West End Community, Inc., and they are now the contractual partner with Durham Parks and Recreation. The DDNP was a background partner in the development of this vibrant community center, which now houses Headstart classrooms, a community health clinic, CommUNITY Scholars (a Project HOPE afterschool program), an active seniors program, arts programming, and Durham Parks and Recreation programs. It is a dynamic community center that is busy and open every day, and it is a testament to the strength of collaborative partnerships. Based on its example, the city of Durham has recently renovated a former neglected middle school into a community center complex. Like Lyon Park, the Holton Recreation Center houses a health clinic and afterschool job development and Parks and Recreation programs. Another new community center is being built in the Walltown neighborhood and is scheduled to open in 2010. The neighborhood stabilization envisioned by the early DDNP collaborative partnership has gained considerable momentum and is rippling through other impoverished Durham neighborhoods.

UNIVERSITY IMPACTS

As noted previously, a strategic goal of the DDNP was to increase the quality and quantity of the "touches" between Duke and the Durham community. An initial priority was to increase trust levels between Durham community residents and Duke University faculty and students. Mary Duke Biddle Trent Semans stated in her recent interview that, although Duke had long been active in the community, its activities were not well-coordinated or visible. John Burness affirmed that although Duke's engagement certainly contained elements of "enlightened self-interest, the work of the DDNP was not public relations." As the university became more engaged in its collaborative partnerships, its positive "touches" began to have a reciprocal benefit, with connections and sustained relationships growing between community and university participants. This has been particularly evident in the work of Duke students in the community.

The CAPD/Marga and Rensselaerville Institute reports found notable accomplishments in the area of university impacts by providing

- a variety of enrichments to DDNP schools and strengthening schools from a variety of campus resources; and
- additional services to DDNP neighborhoods, such as legal counsel for nonprofit organizations, pastoral counseling for local residents, health services, and financial assessments.

Components of university engagement that worked well included:

- collaboration from a variety of Duke departments, including medicine, law, engineering, business, divinity, campus and auxiliary services such as facilities management, Duke University stores, and dining services;
- creating courses, clinics, and programs in response to student demand;
- training students *before* they engaged with neighborhood organizations;
- utilizing external funding sources and leveraging resources from a variety of sources;
- using the DDNP to help Duke personnel connect effectively with community partners;
- incorporating into the student curriculum an approach that holds everyone more accountable; and
- utilizing social entrepreneurs who have developed successful projects to attract students and sustain attendance in project activities.

Challenges requiring further work noted by the two reports were:

- developing a comprehensive set of indicators to benchmark university engagement;
- getting financial commitments from departments or schools;
- matching department funding with foundation resources;

- matching unique resource needs with university personnel;
- achieving continuity of programming when students are involved;
- lessening the disconnect between faculty and Durham residents;
- eliminating the community's perception that they are being used as a laboratory; and
- sharing research findings effectively with community residents.

By 2007, the two major sources of civic engagement funding, the Kellogg Foundation and Fund for the Improvement of Postsecondary Education (FIPSE) grants, were ending. As the FIPSE grant wound down, Robert Thompson, the dean of Trinity College, stepped in and provided a budget to support the development of the Office of Service Learning. This office now functions within the overall university to support the development of service-learning courses by Duke faculty and to consult with faculty on the logistics of program administration. The Office of Service Learning also coordinates regular meetings and workshops for interested faculty members. This assists in the development of an internal faculty cohort for the discussion of problems and solutions to service-learning concerns. David Malone noted in his interview that major accomplishments of the service-learning movement included:

- the involvement of more than 600 students Durham Public Schools and community centers;
- a sense of institutional long-term commitment, now involving many other offices and departments; and
- the development of relationships within Durham that have strengthened as partners continue programs and work together to navigate collaborative program administration.

Service-learning opportunities conducted in afterschool program settings have many advantages for community partners, university students, and university faculty and staff. Through university tutors, mentors, and activity volunteers, community partners gain access to free and energetic volunteer assistance in the management of their programs. With coordinated training and supervision, service-learning students are a creative resource for community programs. Reciprocally, the intermediary space provided by afterschool programs and other community settings operate as a safe space for university students and community youth to interact and learn from one another. Community youth are able to take advantage of the knowledge and experience that these older peers can provide, using creative methods that benefit from a common peer culture. University students are often challenged to learn strategies for translating what they know into formats that will assist community youth in more effective learning. Practice working within culturally diverse settings assists both community youth and university students in expanding their range of cultural competencies.

Expanding cultural competency becomes an adult learning task as well for community partners and university personnel. The multiple tasks of program administration, such as organizing service-learning opportunities and evaluation procedures, forces university and community partners into continuous communication and relationships. Program success is built upon the reflective infrastructure of these relationships. Partnerships across cultural boundaries require the courage to take risks, admit mistakes, and identify problems, as well as the resilience to make the effort to respond, reflect, and adapt as necessary to ensure success. This is a challenging task, requiring an attitude that is constructive and willing to go beyond normal practice and working hours.

Another significant aspect of community impacts on the university has been the broad development of student outreach projects and organizations. Over the last decade, students have unleashed their entrepreneurial skills with multiple projects and initiatives targeting local, national, and global problems. Although student groups emerge from a wide range of sources, they receive primary infrastructure support from three university offices: Student Affairs, the Center for Civic Engagement, and the Office of Community Affairs. Individual departments or programs may also sponsor student groups committed to social action.

Dr. Sam Miglarese, director of Community Engagement for the Office of Community Affairs, notes that students are the third leg of community impacts. He states that they are a source of influence and power, but benefit from the infrastructure support of the university to guide their efforts to effective programs. Courses in public policy, such as those developed by Professor Anthony Brown, were instrumental in assisting students to turn their ideas into concrete, sustained programming. Office of Community Affairs staff such as Dr. Miglarese facilitate the community interaction and infrastructure support needed for student outreach projects to be productive and sustainable. The resource chart in Chapter 2 (Table 2.1) lists notable examples of successful academic support and mentoring programs, such the Girls Club, CLICK, and Project Child. Other projects address specific skill interests such as WOODS (outdoor recreation), Swim with the Blue Devils, and Club Tennis.

One initiative, Student U, is its own nonprofit organization and was designed and implemented by a Duke student, Dan Kimberg. Student U was developed as an undergraduate project and is currently thriving as an intensive academic support program for Durham middle school students. Student U recruits students from Duke, University of North Carolina–Chapel Hill, and North Carolina Central University to teach in its 8-week summer program and follow-up academic-year mentoring programs. A course supporting the work of the teachers is jointly taught by faculty from the University of North Carolina, Duke, and North Carolina Central University faculty. Student U now reaches 150 Durham middle school students each year and is just one example among many of what is possible when talented undergraduates receive grounding and infrastructure support from their host university.

Duke graduate and professional schools have also developed long-standing commitments with community partners. Duke's law clinic provides legal counsel at reduced rates to community members on a variety of legal issues. The law clinic has also worked with Office of Community Affairs to design contracts that contain the flexibility and structure for secure legal arrangements with community partners. Fuqua School of Business regularly uses its social entrepreneurship internships to collaborate on community projects. Vital planning for a major streetscape renovation was conducted by business school interns. Duke medical residents regularly volunteer healthy habits and dental care workshops in schools and afterschool programs. The Center for Documentary Studies routinely works with community partners to develop community arts projects, audio and video documentaries that chronicle neighborhood stories and community events.

A notable feature of Duke University's structural organization has long been its emphasis on its interdisciplinary approaches to academics and outreach projects. Outreach to neighboring universities has increased in the past decade and has been the source of several programming successes. The work of the DDNP has contributed to cross-institutional efforts on projects with Durham community partners. A local charter school, Carter Community School, benefited for several years from collaboration with the Robertson Scholars program. Robertson Scholars are drawn from both the University of North Carolina-Chapel Hill and Duke University campuses, with community service locally and abroad as a major feature of their scholarship program. Robertson Scholars worked with Carter Community School staff to develop and implement enrichment programming that the school was unable to afford for its students. Scholars provided recreational activities on a rotating basis each week for Carter students. Arts enrichment is now a signature focus of the Carter Community School and Duke's Arts Engagement program, which is organized by Duke arts faculty and their students and sponsored by the Office of the Vice Provost for the Arts, the Program in Education, and the Office of Service Learning.

The SWCD Quality of Life project also became the site for cross-institutional engagement and collaboration among University of North Carolina–Chapel Hill and North Carolina State University social work, urban planning, and architecture students and community residents on a number of neighborhood improvement projects. The improvement projects were identified by the community residents involved with the Quality of Life Program. When Ms. Webb-Bledsoe realized that Duke did not have the social work or planning resources the project needed, she contacted other universities to enlist their support. Along with Duke's Fuqua School of Business, the Quality of Life Project was able to plan and submit for city approval a major streetscape planning project. The project would involve major redevelopment of one of the main thoroughfares in this neighborhood and also a main artery leading to Duke's campus.

In a similar fashion, the afterschool programs followed the lead established by the school health clinics to work closely with the Center for Child and Family Mental Health. The center was a collaboration of Duke, the University of North Carolina–Chapel Hill, and North Carolina Central University aimed at supporting the mental health needs of Durham children and their families. The agency provided social work and clinical assessment services to the schools and afterschool programs. For several years, a team of social workers and an education specialist worked with the afterschool programs to promote positive health habits and prosocial skills. The Kellogg Foundation also funded the Saturday Academy of North Carolina Central University for 5 years. As a result of working together on these programs, Duke and North Carolina Central University won a 21st Century Community Learning Centers grant, which they jointly administered for 4 years. This grant allowed for expanded afterschool programs in the neighborhoods immediately surrounding the North Carolina Central University campus and an additional afterschool program in the DDNP.

Following the lacrosse incident, Duke and North Carolina Central University students made a decision to work together across their respective campus organizations to promote joint activities between the two campuses. This response to the specific incident and the long history of segregated campuses has resulted in cross-campus dialogue and the planning of joint social events such as Duke–North Carolina Central University games and community service activities. These acts of sharing events and working together help to build the cross-institutional bonds and infrastructure necessary to reduce racial divisions and social segregation.

The accomplishments of the first decade, while extensive, have been difficult to chronicle. As noted in the reports, each area needs to continue working on developing benchmarks for determining adequate results. This will provide confirming evidence of the work being done in each strategic goal area. Each club, outreach project, and service-learning course has a story, and every story has a widening effect of reciprocal impacts between the university and community partners. The tentative bridges that were so painstakingly constructed in the early years of the DDNP now have an increasing volume of traffic. The early dream of building the quality and quantity of university–community touches has merged into a daily reality for Durham residents and Duke University faculty, staff and students.

UNIVERSITY ADMINISTRATIVE PRIORITIES AND CHALLENGES

A university may appear to be a monolithic organization, when the reality is quite different. It's fundamentally a decentralized institution with complex, competing priorities often isolated in departments, centers, and institutes. Sustaining resource support for the goals of the university–community partnership requires the drive of internal and external forces. A combination of 2 years' worth of internal strategic planning and the external evaluation reports of 2006 and 2008 resulted in further organization changes for the DDNP.

On September 14, 2006, Duke University's Board of Trustees adopted a new strategic plan for the university, titled "Making a Difference: The Strategic Plan for Duke University." Included in the plan was further integration of the DDNP into the university's long-term goals:

> We commit to continuing to build the programs in the Neighborhood Partnership, with particular emphasis on K–12 education and youth development, neighborhood stabilization, support for our non-profit partners, and engagement of Duke students in the life of Durham. (Making a Difference report, p. 61)

John Burness, the longtime senior vice president for Government Relations and Public Affairs retired in June 2008. He was succeeded by Dr. Phail Wynn, who was retiring from his long tenure as president of Durham Technical Community College. A new office was formed, the Office of Durham and Regional Affairs (DARA), and Dr. Wynn was named its vice president. DARA is responsible for the Office of Community Affairs and the newly determined strategic goals of broadening the university's role as an advocate for economic and community development in Durham and the region. DARA's goals are to continue

- the economic partnership with the City of Durham in order to attract and maintain local business that will increase employment, broaden the tax base, and establish downtown Durham as an attractive retail destination;
- the partnership with the Manpower Development Corporation in developing a comprehensive support system for disconnected youth in Durham;
- using research to develop new education initiatives with Durham Public Schools;
- developing regional partnerships to ensure future innovation and economic growth in the region; and
- expanding collaboration with Duke faculty, staff, and students to strengthen and build the capacity of nonprofit community partners.

The broader systemic goals reflected in these goals is a shift from the narrower, contained neighborhood focus of the DDNP's first decade. The work of the DDNP and its Office of Community Affairs continues and functions as a part of the larger goals of the DARA office.

An immediate and unforeseen change faced by this expanded focus has been the financial downturn of 2008–2009. Duke University, like many other universities, faced significant financial difficulties from the challenging financial environment. University requests for budget trimming combined with expanded strategic goals placed inevitable stresses on available resources. Community partners, too, faced concerns about their ability to sustain programming in the light of administrative priority shifts, stretched financial resources, and university staffing commitments.

A further external pressure stemmed from increased accountability and evaluation requirements from funding sources. Major funders are changing their priorities from project-based development to larger systemic involvement with more formal evaluation requirements. Given the concerns stated in Chapter 4 regarding the difficulties of conducting formal evaluation procedures in community-based settings with limited resources, the challenge and value of university–community partnerships is increased. The work with afterschool programs is a good example of the challenges. Few afterschool programs have the secure funding base and professional training to fully participate in rigorous experimental design models. The flexible and fluid nature of afterschool programs is an exciting arena for exploring research techniques that assist the social sciences in understanding how to "prepare the ground" or develop interim documentation of successful program practices. Accepting the current state of the field and using research expertise which can work in community settings is a critical need for the field. This has applicability far beyond the limited and supplementary role of afterschool programs.

Another complement to the possibilities of reframing and developing useful research strategies for community settings is expanding the capacities of CBOs. Formative evaluation techniques, which allow collaborative partnerships to learn and bring everyone along in the process, increase the overall community capacity for reflection, documentation, and program improvement. Evaluation becomes a necessary tool to the common task of improving positive youth development in our respective communities. The perception of the community as a laboratory and its residents as "lab rats" is diminished.

A dialogue between funders, CBOs and evaluators is needed to devise more realistic evaluation frameworks and funding cycles. Reflecting upon the extensive evaluation process that was formatively managed within Project HOPE, the process took from Year 1 to Year 3 to have a fully functioning infrastructure and to develop effective strategies that were genuinely reflective of program practice. We were fortunate to have external evaluators who were patient guides in all aspects of the process and who were able to attract the additional funding necessary to continue our evaluation procedures. The long-term value this represents is that Project HOPE now has a longitudinal database on its afterschool programs that allows us to disseminate our experiences to the field through consultation, conference papers, workshops, and publications.

Sustained, productive university and community partnerships require increasing the quantity and quality of faculty engagement. The increase of service-learning courses to its current level of 49 courses across a growing number of Duke departments is a positive sign of faculty interest in creating coursework with a strong service-learning component. A more difficult challenge is to link service learning to disciplinary pedagogy and faculty research goals. Not every discipline lends itself easily to community-based work, although, with some creativity, there undoubtedly are more opportunities than our traditional academic culture currently supports. Finally, a broadening of what is considered acceptable research for the university's promotion and tenure process would assist in supporting increased faculty engagement. A tolerance for less conventional research methods, topics, and processes is necessary to encourage program experimentation and innovation. Ultimately, there must be a "goodness of fit" between the teaching and research goals of the university and university–community partnership goals.

CONCLUSION—WHERE DO WE GO FROM HERE?

Duke University, while facing many challenges in the years ahead, has come a long way in its development of a sustained, productive university and community partnership. This progress was recognized most notably on February 11, 2008, when Duke University was named "with distinction" to the second annual President's Higher Education Community Service Honor Roll. The honor roll recognizes higher education institutions that support "innovative, effective, and exemplary community service programs" (Duke Today, Feburary, 19, 2008). Also in 2008, Duke became enrolled in the Carnegie Community Engagement Classification. Duke was classified in both Curricular Engagement and Outreach Partnership. This is an elective process designed for the purpose of promoting institutional self-assessment and reflection. The two applications for these awards were prepared and submitted by Elaine Madison, associate director of DukeEngage, and Rev. Dr. Sam Miglarese, DDNP director of Community Engagement.

Duke continues to broaden its community service goals. Duke Engage, an innovative summer internship program funded by the Gates Foundation and Duke University, was launched in 2007. Under the direction of Dr. Eric Mlyn, the program places several hundred Duke undergraduates in immersion community service projects locally, nationally, and internationally. Duke undergraduates work closely with faculty for 8 weeks each summer on targeted service projects. These internships range from local services evaluating housing lead levels or water quality testing to developing a middle school for girls in East Africa. Students are encouraged to continue taking coursework and conducting research studies upon their return to campus each fall.

In August of 2009, Duke's Program in Education became the International Association for Research on Service-Learning and Community Engagement. According to Dr. Jan Riggsbee, director of the Program in Education, this recently formed organization seeks to develop an international cohort of universities and colleges engaged in promoting service-learning on their respective campuses. The universities plan to conduct collaborative research and support one another and are currently making plans for the next international conference in 2012.

The careful work of putting together programming that responded to genuine community needs has more than met its foundation goal of improving the quantity and quality of "touches" within Durham. The bottom line of university–community partnerships becomes, "Is all of this effort worth it?" As detailed in this book, partnerships required an intense combination of individuals with the passion, talent, and skills for working in communities with rich histories, complex social networks, and significant issues requiring real solutions. One conclusion is that universities need to be prepared for the long-term investments of time, energy, resources, and personnel that are necessary for this work to be successful. Although it's important to proceed carefully and perhaps to begin with smaller, more manageable projects while learning the ropes of program administration, the effort cannot be partial, part-time, or something that is done in one's spare time. Anything less than authentic engagement will be read by community residents as a manipulative public relations event or a well-meaning but typically clueless effort that does more harm than good.

The journey beyond the campus wall remains a challenge with each step taking us out of the security of the campus or neighborhood environments. Collectively, is it worth it? This is a question that present and future university and community residents will have to answer. What will it take to answer affirmatively? Some generic questions to consider when evaluating partnerships are:

- How many at-risk students are being promoted and graduating?
- How many tutors are participating, and how many tutoring hours are being spent?
- How many afterschool programs and lists of enrichment activities are there?

- How many homes have been built and renovated?
- How many children and adults are receiving health care?
- How many community centers are thriving?
- How many valued, trusting relationships are there between community residents and university students, faculty, and staff?
- How do we measure the longer term benefits that we cannot now foresee?
- What is the tipping point that defines the success of a university–community partnership and makes it worth the long-term, sustained investment of talent and treasure?

These are questions that this book can contribute to, but not fully answer. What we can answer are the initial questions posed at the beginning of the book from the perspectives and experiences of the DDNP. It is the hope of this study that these answers will contribute to the conversations and future work of university–community partnerships.

What can community-based afterschool programs do to promote positive youth development with low-income minority youth? When the DDNP first launched Project HOPE in 2002, there was scant evidence to indicate the efficacy of community-based afterschool programs promoting positive youth development for low-income minority students. Research studies, large and small, now confirm the academic and social benefits of afterschool programs (Fabiano et al., 2006; Hirsch, 2005; Little, Wimer, & Weiss, 2008; Vandell et al., 2007). Afterschool programs have proved to be of special importance to low-income youth, who may not have the access to academic support and enrichment activities in their communities. Project HOPE's evaluation data further confirm these research findings. Participating students consistently demonstrate academic and social gains when students have access to a wide range of enrichment activities. Afterschool programs in Durham have expanded and are now available in school settings, recreation centers, housing projects, and churches. The community and its university partners have witnessed the evidence of student achievement and are demanding more afterschool programs in a wide range of school and community settings. Community-based afterschool programs have proven their capacity to positively impact the lives of the children in their neighborhoods and are worth the time, talent, and resources necessary to support their effective functioning.

How do we successfully manage a collaborative university and community partnership with the complex requirements of joint program administration? Joint program administration was undoubtedly the most difficult aspect of the university–community partnership in the beginning, but was also a highly rewarding aspect of the collaboration. Project HOPE's initial collaborative work came on the heels of a prior unsuccessful university–community project, so virtually every aspect of the early project development was tested for its authenticity and service delivery aspects. Successful program administration required maintaining a balance between providing enough structure to ensure effective program functioning and the flexibility to allow individual program autonomy. Establishing clear roles and responsibilities and engendering responsive communication were key elements to setting up the partnership. Consistent service delivery and fiscal management strategies assisted in the evolution of a sound programming infrastructure. Providing support when and where it was needed led to the development of trust between project personnel and to effective problem-solving strategies. The afterschool site coordinators had the best sense for what worked in their settings with their available resources. Project staff had the capacity to provide information about best practices and what program components were necessary to ensure program quality. While complex, it was also an approach that combined the strengths of the university and community partners while minimizing the weaknesses of each organization. When a collaboration of this nature works well, it has a positive dynamic that produces results and benefits beyond expectation. For Project HOPE and the DDNP generally, this approach has been highly successful, so the answer to this second question is affirmative. However, the area of university–community administration is one that still requires further study, implementation, and sharing of best practices. Significant challenges remain in sustaining university and community programming, including leadership and personnel changes, sustained funding, and the alignment of programs with academic priorities and research interests.

Who learns and what is learned? The answer to this question is, remarkably, *everyone learns!* While we can discuss generic categories of what may be learned by participants, the content of what is learned varies by coursework, activities, and the individual's learning proclivities. Primary learners for Project HOPE were certainly the Durham student participants of the afterschool programs and their Duke student tutors. Student participants learned academic skills, study habits, and positive social skills through the tutoring and mentoring provided by their older peer tutors and community adults. Through their coursework and experiential learning, Duke students learned to bridge theory and practice. They experienced the frustrations of problem-based learning and the satisfactions of working through problems to a solution that benefited another person. They developed cultural competencies as they negotiated diverse settings and worked collaboratively with multiple partners.

Community partners and university project staff probably learned more from each other than they may have expected. Community partners gained access to research and best practice models. When questions arose, they had ready access to university staff and resources. University personnel learned from their community partners the history and social experiences of the sites where they were working. Behind the door of every vacant house and building in the neighborhood, there's a story. Learning from those stories changed the assumptions and perspectives of the community project experience. Faculty research possibilities and opportunities for collaboration expanded. There is no shortage of ideas and projects that could benefit from further research and program development.

Finally, the university learns from expanding its parameters to institutionally support the programs, coursework, and research opportunities presented by university–community partnerships. Fundamentally, the university learns what works and what doesn't with collaborative partnerships. Again, assumptions are challenged, perspectives shift, and more effective practices emerge from the application of ideas to real world settings. By sustaining an innovative research and practice loop, the university directly contributes to effective problem solving. Knowledge in the service of society is the broad strategic goal that invites university administration, faculty, and staff to engage in individual and collective exploration of ideas, innovative approaches, and research practices. From their experience with partnerships, programs, and research, universities have the capacity for strategic infrastructure and resource development. Rather than being an isolated and insular campus, the university sustains its societal leadership role and sets a powerful model for community citizenship.

How do we create a culture of evaluation? Working *with* community partners to create a culture of evaluation is an area with the greatest potential for mistrust and suspicion. It is also the area with the best potential for program improvement and for long-term program sustainability. In a research-savvy community like Durham, residents are sensitive to anything that is labeled "research" and are reluctant to be viewed as "research subjects." Evaluation works best when it is undertaken with community partners and developed from the beginning with their full knowledge and input. Once underway, data collection processes require training and support that is cognizant of the partner skill continuum. As data are used for program improvement practices that have direct benefits for their participants, community partners often become enthusiastic contributors to the evaluation process. Efficient, consistent data collection and evaluation are equally appreciated by funding sources who need accountability for their expenditures. Establishing a quantitative and qualitative record of accomplishment is mutually beneficial to all partners.

Universities have the capacity to lend the skills of their trained research staff to create an evaluation culture in the community that understands and has the skills necessary to provide documentation of their program achievements. Developing research practices that will work effectively in community settings and support the research goals of university staff is a challenging but worthwhile goal for university and community partnerships.

What is necessary to sustain programs? Program sustainability is an especially thorny issue for afterschool programming and many other university–community outreach efforts. Once the programs move beyond the start-up funding years, the hunt for long-term operational funding dollars becomes more difficult. Neither government nor foundation cycles are designed for the long-term financial commitment that these programs require. The low-income students being served by these programs have limited capability to manage even a sliding scale fee structure for this type of enrichment programming. Universities can assist in the fiscal planning that program sustainability requires. This may involve direct involvement through advisory board development, grant-writing expertise, and endowment and fund-raising campaigns that utilize university development resources.

Another critical piece of sustainability is the institutional absorption of strategic goals, funding, and personnel resources. Administrative and faculty commitment to stated strategic goals and specific program activities embed university–community partnerships in the mission, curriculum, and activities of the university and reinforce critical, sustained commitments with community partners. Establishing congruence and alignment with the university's mission, strategic goals, and public service ambitions creates the virtuous cycle necessary for a dynamic university–community partnership. Well-established patterns of community good citizenship become, over time, the healthy habits necessary for sustaining beneficial reciprocal relationships.

Can programming be replicated in other communities? The DDNP has been fortunate enough to witness widening impact throughout Durham and the surrounding region. Afterschool programs have been embraced by the community and have been expanded to new recreation centers, churches, and housing projects. Every other programming area—housing, health clinics, and cultural and recreation activities—is being replicated in other impoverished Durham neighborhoods. A ride through Durham's downtown yields a view of a revitalized restaurant, business, housing, and cultural scene that is a lesson in the value of university–community partnerships. Although the collaborative patterns of working together on common problems have somewhat minimized the impact of the economic downturn on Duke–Durham planning initiatives, there remains no guarantee that this investment strategy will continue.

The DDNP staff works with the faculty and Duke departments to disseminate information about its community partnership work. Multiple staff have taken an active role in the North Carolina Campus Compact, participating in conferences and presenting proposals about its collaborative work. Conference presentations and consulting work with other universities have been integrated into the regular work of each DDNP staff member. It's difficult to quantify the impact this has had on the field, but it can be noted that this solid, ongoing contribution to the discussion of university–partnership work has had only positive results.

How does university–community engagement change universities, communities, and student participants? At this point, we've asked and answered fundamental questions about university–community partnerships. Can these partnerships actually make a difference? Is it worth the effort? From the experiences of Duke University and the DDNP, both of these questions can be answered affirmatively and with results-oriented benchmarks and evaluation data. The second question—how are universities, communities, and student participants changed?—is more difficult to answer.

President Richard Brodhead noted several important lessons for university–community partnerships in a recent interview. First, a university ignores its surrounding city at its own peril. Second, life gets more interesting when you stretch your mind outside your own walls. He felt this was particularly important for undergraduates, who are being prepared for the life they will lead in the future. Finally, when you work in partnership, it is required that you spend some time listening as well as talking. For the DDNP, the evidence of these changes is everywhere: improved housing stock; new neighborhood clinics and recreation centers; improved school facilities; the establishment of science and computer labs; and Duke students, faculty, and staff contributing to projects throughout the community. Other changes occur more quietly. Comments from community members about Duke's work in the community mean more than receiving awards. Afterschool site coordinators clamoring for specific Duke tutors (the best ones!) and staying *after* meetings to share ideas about their work speaks volumes. There is still much work to be done. Every need outlined in the original partner matrix still exists—the student achievement gap, access to affordable housing and health care, crime management, and increased engagement with the university. The difference is that now we know *how* to address these problems together with all aspects of the community engaged in discussing and implementing the solutions. We have examples of how this can be done and people who can provide the necessary guidance to implement successful programming. We have the infrastructure to support and sustain future initiatives. The problems are owned and worked on by everyone in full acknowledgement of the common good.

President Brodhead (2010) recalled a welcoming community event that he attended early in his presidency at the Community Family Life and Recreation Center at Lyon Park. The warmth and services provided to community residents at the renovated community center were a clear example of a successful university–community partnership model. He stated that

> when people come back here 5 or 40 years from now, Durham will be famous for a city that, partly through partnership with Duke and partly through other community assets, put together an active presence in neighborhoods where education and health were treated not as luxuries but as the most everyday of needs. (Interview)

Appendix A

ENROLLMENT FORM, ENGLISH

Name: _____ Social Security Number _____

Date of Birth _____ Race _____ Sex (M/F) _____

Address _____ Apt. #_____

City _____ State _____ Zip Code _____

School _____ Teacher _____ Grade _____

Eligible for Free/Reduced Meals? (Y/N)____ Exceptional Child Status (Y/N) _____

Name of Parent/Legal Guardian _____

Work Phone _____ Home Phone _____

Name of Parent/Legal Guardian _____

Work Phone _____ Home Phone _____

Are you currently employed by Duke University? (Y/N) _____ Department _____

Emergency Contact and Relationship _____

Work Phone _____ Home Phone _____

Doctor's Name _____ Doctor's Phone _____

My child has permission to attend field trips sponsored by the tutorial program.

_____ Yes _____ No

The tutorial program has permission to photograph my child.

_____ Yes _____ No

I authorize the tutorial program to transport my child or authorize transportation for my child to a medical facility to be treated in the event of an emergency.

_____ Yes _____ No

By signing below, I grant permission for my child to be enrolled in the tutorial program. My signature confirms that the information provided is accurate.

Parent Signature _____ Date _____

ENROLLMENT FORM, SPANISH

Formulario De Inscripción

Nombre _____ Número de Seguro Social ____-____-____

Fecha de Nacimiento ___/___/___ (mes/día/año) Raza _____ Sexo (M/F) _____

Dirección _____ Número de Apartamento _____

Ciudad _____ Estado _____ Código Postal _____

Escuela _____ Maestro/a _____ Grado _____

¿Elegible para comidas gratis/ precio reducido? (Sí/ No) _____

Recibe Servicios especiales (Sí/ No) _____

Nombre del Padre/ Tutor Legal _____

Teléfono del Trabajo _____ Teléfono de la Casa _____

Nombre de la Madre/ Tutora Legal _____

Teléfono del Trabajo _____ Teléfono de la Casa _____

Contacto en caso de emergencia y parentesco de este _____

Teléfono del Trabajo _____ Teléfono de la Casa _____

Nombre del Doctor _____ Teléfono del Doctor _____

Mi niño/a tiene permiso de asistir a viajes educativos patrocinados por el programa de tutoría.

Sí _____ No _____

Otorgo permiso al programa de tutoría de fotografiar a mi niño/a.

Sí _____ No _____

Otorgo permiso al programa de tutoría para transportar a mi niño/a o autorizo que mi niño/a sea transportado a un edificio médico para ser atendido en caso de una emergencia.

Sí _____ No _____

Al firmar aquí abajo, le doy permiso a mi niño/a para que sea inscrito/a en el programa de tutoría. Mi firma confirma que la información proveída es exacta.

Firma del Padre _____ Fecha _____ (mes/día/año)

Appendix B

PARENT PERMISSION FORM, ENGLISH

Dear Parents,

The afterschool program your child is attending is a Duke–Durham Neighborhood Partnership (DDNP) Afterschool Tutoring Program site. The DDNP Afterschool Tutoring Program provides tutoring programs for your afterschool program, with Duke University students working as tutors. The Duke tutor will help your child with their homework, reading, math, or writing activities for about an hour two times a week.

The tutoring experience is voluntary and your child may choose to stop at any time. We will do all we can to ensure that your child has a pleasant and success-ful learning experience. Since your child's health and well being are our primary concern, Duke tutors are legally required to report any suspected child abuse to the appropriate authorities.

The afterschool and DDNP Afterschool Tutoring Program staff will want to know if what they are doing is helping your child do better in school. In order to do this, we need your permission to monitor your child's attendance, report card, end-of-grade testing scores, Individualized Education Program information, if any, and to communicate with the classroom teacher/s during the 2009–10 school year. At no time will your child's name appear with their grades, end-of-grade scores or attendance records, nor will this information be shared with others. At the beginning and end of the school year, the afterschool staff will ask you to complete a parent satisfaction survey that will take no more than 5 minutes. Completion of the survey is voluntary and your responses will be kept confidential.

Please feel free to contact me at 668-6276 if you have any questions about the DDNP Afterschool Tutoring Program and its study. If you have any further questions about your child's rights as a participant in the DDNP Afterschool Tutoring Program study, please contact the chair of the Human Subjects Committee at 684-3030.

Thank you,

Dr. Barbara C. Jentleson

DDNP Afterschool Tutoring Program Director

____ I give permission for the DDNP Afterschool Tutoring Program to collect my child's attendance, report card, IEP, EOG testing scores. and to communicate with classroom teacher(s). I understand that this information will be used only for pro-gram evaluation purposes.

Student Name _____

Parent/Guardian Signature _____Date:_____

PARENT PERMISSION FORM, SPANISH

Estimados Padres,

El programa de después de clases al cual su niño/a está asistiendo forma parte del Programa de Tutoria de Duke–Durham Partnership. El Programa de tutoria de Duke–Durham Partnership provee programas de tutoría en el marco de su programa de después de clases, con estudiantes de la Universidad de Duke trabajando como tutores. El tutor de Duke le ayudará a su niño/a con su tarea, lectura, matemáticas o actividades de escritura a razón de una hora dos veces por semana.

La experiencia de tutoría es voluntaria y su niño/a puede decidir pararla cuando lo desee. Vamos a hacer todo lo posible para asegurarnos que su niño/a tenga una experiencia de aprendizaje agradable y exitosa. Como la salud y bienestar de su niño/a es nuestra prioridad, los tutores de Duke están obligados legalmente de reportar cualquier sospecha de abuso a las autoridades apropiadas.

El personal de después de clases y el Programa deTutoria de Duke–Durham Partnership desearán averiguar si lo que están haciendo le está ayudando a su niño/a a mejorar su rendimiento escolar. Para poder hacer esto, necesitamos su permiso para monitorear la asistencia de su niño/a, su boletín de notas, su plan de educacion individualizado (IEP), si las hay, y comunicarnos con su maestro de clase durante el año escolar 2009-10. En ningún momento el nombre de su niño/a aparecerá junto a su grado, resultados de los EOG o record de asistencia, ni tampoco se compartirá dicha información con otras personas. Las Escuelas Públicas de Durham no están conduciendo ni patrocinando esta investigación. No habrá ninguna penalización para usted o su niño/a si usted decide no participar en esta investigación. Al principio y al final del año escolar, el personal de después de clase le pedirá que llene una encuesta sobre la satisfacción de los padres. Dicha encuesta no tomará más de 5 minutos. El hecho de contestar a la encuesta es voluntario y sus respuestas se mantendrán confidenciales.

Si usted tiene preguntas sobre el Programa de Tutoria de Duke–Durham Partnership y este estudio, por favor comuníquese conmigo al 668-6276. Si tiene más preguntas sobre los derechos de su niño/a como participante en el estudio del Programa de Tutoria de Duke–Durham Partnership, por favor comuníquese con el Presidente del Comité de Investigación sobre Sujeto Humano al 684-3030.

Gracias,

Dra. Barbara C. Jentleson,

Directora, Programa de Tutoria de Duke–Durham Partnership

____ Le doy permiso al Programa de Tutoria de Duke–Durham Partnership para recopilar la asistencia de mi niño/a, su boletín de notas, IEP, sus resultados en los exámenes de final de año (EOG) y communicarse con su maestro de clase. Entiendo que toda esta información se utilizará solamente para propósitos de evaluación del programa.

Nombre dele studiante:_____

Padre/Tutor Firma _____ Fecha _____

Appendix C

PROJECT HOPE—LOGIC MODEL

Revised: March 3, 2006

Discussion: The activities listed in this logic model represent the general range of activities that may be offered by Project HOPE during the period that the program operates. Some activities may be incorporated from the beginning of the program, other activities may be phased in over several years. In addition, some activities are more relevant to certain age groups and therefore should be directed toward a subset of all students.

Activities	Outputs	Short-term and Intermediate Outcomes
A. Major Outcome: Increased Academic Achievement		
In order to address our objective, we will conduct the following activities: 1. Recruit student tutors for programs. 2. Conduct orientation and training of tutors. 3. Conduct tutoring sessions for the students. 4. Monitor tutoring activities throughout semester. 5. Conduct workshops in study skills and work habits (unless this is already included in tutoring sessions).	The activities will produce the following evidence of service delivery: 1. Number and percent of students participating in Project HOPE programs. 2. Number of tutors working with students. 3. Number of tutoring hours. 4. Number of students participating in Saturday Academy. 5. Number and percent of students and parents expressing satisfaction with the program. 6. Number and percent of tutors expressing satisfaction with the program. 7. Number and percent of students participating in Project HOPE programs (tutoring, social and life skills, career development, and other activities) from year 1 to year 2, year 2 to year 3, etc.	We expect that as a result of participation in program activities, students will experience the following changes in knowledge, skills, attitudes, and behavior: 1. Students maintain and/or improve school attendance rates. 2. Students improve study skills and work habits. 3. Students improve reading and math skills. 4. Students maintain and/or improve GPA. 5. Students maintain and/or improve EOG test scores.

Activities	Outputs	Short-term and Intermediate Outcomes
B. Major Outcome: Enhanced Life Skills		
In order to address our objective, we will conduct the following activities: 1. Offer a social and life skills curriculum. 2. Offer community-based mentoring to foster stable relationships with caring adults. 3. Involve students in community service projects. 4. Conduct arts enrichment activities for students. 5. Conduct recreational programs for students. 6. Conduct community field trips for students. 7. Offer Saturday Academy enrichment activities. 8. Provide health education training and health service support for students.	The activities will produce the following evidence of service delivery: 1. Number and percent of students participating in each of the activities. 2. Number of community-based mentors. 3. Number and percent of students receiving health education training. 4. Number of students receiving health services.	We expect that as a result of participation in program activities, students will experience the following changes in knowledge, skills, attitudes, and behavior: 1. Students demonstrate improved attitudes toward school and academic activities. 2. Students demonstrate positive relationships with peers/adults. 3. Students are involved in their school and community. 4. Students develop healthy lifestyle choices.
C. Major Outcome: Improved Career Development		
In order to address our objective, we will conduct the following activities: 1. Provide technology skills training to students. 2. Offer career interests/career goal development activities for students, including career-related field trips. 3. Offer activities in job skill development for older students. 4. Place older students in part-time jobs.	The activities will produce the following evidence of service delivery: 1. Number and percent of students participating in technology skills training. 2. Number and percent of students participating in career interests/career goal development activities, including field trips. 3. Number and percent of students participating in job skills development. 4. Number and percent of older students in part-time jobs.	We expect that as a result of participation in program activities, students will experience the following changes in knowledge, skills, attitudes, and behavior: 1. Students indicate an increased use of computers. 2. Students demonstrate increased understanding of the importance of secondary school and post-secondary school planning. 3. Students demonstrate an increased interest in college and/or a career. 4. Students demonstrate improved job skills.

References

Alden, B., interview, January 21, 2009. Durham, NC.

Anderson, E. (1999). *Code of the Street.* New York: W.W. Norton.

Benson, L., Harkavy, I., & Puckett, J. (2007). *Dewey's dream.* Philadelphia: Temple University Press.

Bodilly, S., & Beckett, M. K. (2005). *Making out-of-school time matter.* Santa Monica, CA: Rand Corporation for the Wallace Foundation.

Bok, D. (1990). *Universities and the future of America.* Durham, NC: Duke University Press.

Bouffard, S. (2003). Doing what works: Scientifically based research in education. *Harvard Family Research Project: The Evaluation Exchange, 9*(1).

Bouffard, S., & Little, P. (2003). A review of activity implementation in out-of-school time programs. *Harvard Family Research Project: Out-of-School Time Evaluation Snapshot, 9*(2).

Bouffard, S. M., Wimer, C., Caronogan, P., Little, P. M. D., Dearing, E., & Simpkins, S. D. (2006, May). Demographic differences in patterns of youth out-of-school time activity participation. *Journal of Youth Development, 1*(1).

Boyer, E. (1994). Creating the new American college. *The Chronicle of Higher Education,* March 9, A48.

Bringle, R. G., & Hatcher, J. A. (1999). Reflection in service-learning: Making meaning of experience. *Educational Horizons,* Summer, 179–185.

Burness, J., interview, July 21, 2008. Durham, NC.

Burness, J. (1996). *Duke–Durham community affairs: Building the framework for partnership, progress report.* Durham, NC: Duke University Office of Government Relations and Community Affairs.

Capella, E., & Larner, M. B. (1999). America's schoolchildren: Past, present, and future. *The Future of Children, 9*(2), 21–30.

Chung, A.-M., & Hillsman, E. (2005). Evaluating afterschool programs: Early reports find positive gains but more research still needed. *The School Administrator,* May.

Cooper, C. R., Denner, J., & Lopez, E. (1999). Cultural brokers: Helping Latino children on pathways toward success. *The Future of Children, 9(2),* 51–58.

Cooper, H. (2001). Summer school: Research-based recommendations for policymakers. *SERVE Policy Brief,* 1–8.

Cooper, H., Valentine, J. C., Lindsay, J. L., & Nye, B. (1999). Relationships between five afterschool activities and academic achievement. *Journal of Educational Psychology, 91(2),* 369–378.

_____. (2008, February 18). Duke honored for community service. *Duke Today.* Durham, NC: Duke Office of News and Communication.

Durden, R. F. (1987). *The dukes of Durham, 1865–1929.* Durham, NC: Duke University Press.

Eyler, J., & Giles, D. E. (1999). *Where's the learning in service-learning?* San Francisco, CA: Jossey-Bass.

Fabiano, L., Pearson, L. M., Reisner, E. R., & Williams, I. J. (2006). *Preparing students in the middle grades to succeed in high schools: Findings from Phase IV of the citizen schools evaluation.* Washington, DC: Policy Studies Association.

Fashola, O. S. (2002). *Building effective afterschool pograms.* Thousand Oaks, CA: Corwin Press.

Fleishman, J. (2007). *The foundation: A great American secret, how private wealth is changing the world.* New York: Public Affairs.

Fordham, I. (2004). Out-of-school hours learning in the United Kingdom. In G. Noam (Ed.), *New Directions for Youth Development,* 101, 43–74.

Forum for Youth Investment (2002). Policy commentary #1; Afterschool research meets afterschool policy. Washington, DC: *Forum for Youth Investment.*

Friedman, L. N., & Bleiberg, M. (2002). The long-term sustainability of afterschool programs: The afterschool corporations strategy. In G. Noam & B. M. Miller (Eds.), *New Directions for Youth Development,* 94, 19–39.

Gambone, M. A., Klem, A. M., & Connell, J. P. (2002). *Finding out what matters for youth.* Philadelphia: Youth Development Strategies, Inc., and Institute for Research and Reform in Education.

Garner, R. (Ed.) (2002). *Hanging out.* Westport, CT: Bergin & Garvey.

Halpern, R. (2003). *Making play work*. New York: Teachers College Press.

Halpern, R. (1999). Afterschool programs for low-income children: Promise and challenges. *The Future of Children, 9*(2), 81–96.

Harkavy, I. (1998*). School–community–university partnerships: Effectively integrating community building and education reform.* Paper presented to conference on Connecting Community Building and Education Reform: Effective School, Community, University Partnerships. Washington, DC: U.S. Department of Education and U.S. Department of Housing and Urban Development.

Hirsch, B. J. (2005). *A place to call home*. New York: Teachers College Press.

Huang, D., Coordt, A., LaTorre, D., Leon, S., Miyoshi, J., Perez, P. (2007). The afterschool hours: Examing the relationship between afterschool staff-based social capital and student engagement in LA's BEST. Los Angeles: UCLA/CRESST.

Kakli, Z., Krieder, H., Little, P., Buck, T., & Coffey, M. (2006). *Focus on families! How to build and support family-centered practices in afterschool.* Harvard Family Research Project and Build the Out-of-School Time Network (BOSTnet).

Kerrebrock, N., & Lewitt, E. (1999). Children in self-care. *The Future of Children: When School Is Out. 9*(2), 151–161.

Keohane, N. O., interview, November, 2009. Durham, NC.

Keohane, N. O. (2006). *Higher ground: Ethics and leadership in the modern university.* Durham, NC: Duke University Press.

Lange, P., (2009, January 8). Interview. Durham, NC.

Little, P., Wimer, C., & Weiss (2008). After school programs in the 21st century: Their potential and what it takes to achieve it. *Harvard Family Research Project: Issues and Opportunities in Out-of-School Time Evaluation, 9*(10), Harvard Family Research Project.

Mahoney, J. L., Eccles, J. S., & Larson, R. W. Processes of adjustment in organized out-of-school activities: Opportunities and risk. In G. Noam (Ed.). *New Directions for Youth Development*, 101, 115–144.

Malone, D., interview, November 23, 2009. Durham, NC.

Maurasse, D. (2001). *Beyond the Campus*. New York: Routledge.

Liederman, S., Liederman, M., Maurasse, D., & Jones, C. (2006). *Duke–Durham neighborhood partnership evaluation: A report to the Duke endowment and Duke University.* November, 1, 2006.

Medoff, P., & Sklar, H. (1994). *Streets of HOPE*. Cambridge, MA: South End Press.

Miglarese, S. (2009, October 30). Interview. Durham, NC.

Newman, S. A., Fox, J., Flynn, E., & Christeson, W. (2000). *America's afterschool choice: The prime time for juvenile crime or youth enrichment and achievement.* Washington, DC: Fight Crime: Invest in Kids.

Noam, G., Miller, B. M., & Barry, S. (2002). Youth development and afterschool time: Policy and programming in large cities. In G. Noam (Ed.), *New Directions for Youth Development, 94,* 9–18.

Noam, G., & Tillinger, J. R. (2004). Afterschool as intermediary space: Theory and typology of partnerships. In G. Noam (Ed.). *New Directions for Youth Development, 101,* 75–113.

Palmer, ___. (1009, January 14). Interview. Durham, NC.

Pittman, K., Irby, M., Yahatem, N., & Wilson-Ahlstron, A. (2004). Blurring the lines for learning: The role of out-of-school time programs as complements to formal learning. In G. Noam (Ed.), *New Directions for Youth Development, 101,* p. 19–41.

Ramalay, J. A. (2007). Reflections on the public purposes of higher education. *Wingspread Journal: Beyond the Ivory Tower.* Racine, WI: Johnson Foundation.

Reisner, E. R., White, R. N., Brimingham, J., & Welsh, M. (2001). *Building quality and supporting expansion of Afterschool Projects: Evaluation results from the TASC Afterschool Program's second year.* Washington, DC: Policy Studies Associates.

Riggsbee, J., interview, December 10, 2009. Durham, NC.

Rodin, Judith (2007). *The university and urban revival.* Philadelphia: The University of Pennsylvania Press.

Semans, M. D. B. T., interview, December 3, 2009. Durham, NC.

Spring, Joel (2005). *The American School: 1642–2004* (6th ed.). New York: McGraw-Hill.

Strand, K., Marullo, S., Cutforth, N., Stoeker, R., & Donohue, P. (2003). *Community-based research and higher education.* San Francisco, CA: Jossey-Bass.

Theokas, C., Lerner, J. V., Phelps, E., & Lerner, R. (2006). Cacophony and change in youth afterschool activities: Findings from the 4-H study of positive youth development. *Journal of Youth Development, 1*(1).

Tucker, C. M., & Herman, K. C. (2002). Using culturally sensitive theories and research to meet academic needs of low-income African-American children. *American Psychologist, 57*(10), 762–773.

Upton, J., & Whittington, D. (2007). *Duke University Project HOPE, annual external evaluation report: Program impacts and recommendations.* Powell, OH: Institutional Research Consultants.

Vandell, D. L., & Pierce, K. M. (1998). *Measures used in the study of afterschool care: Psychometric properties and validity information.* Unpublished manuscript, University of Wisconsin–Madison.

Vandell, D., Reisner, E., & Pierce, K. (2007). *Outcomes linked to high-quality afterschool programs: Longitudinal findings from the study of promising practices.* Irvine: University of California and Policy Studies Associates.

Vandell, D., & Shumow, L. (1999). Afterschool child care programs. *Future of Children, 9*(3), 64–80.

Vandivere, S., Tout, K., Capizzano, M. A., & Zaslow, M. (2003, April). Left unsupervised: A look at the most vulnerable children. *Child Trends Research Brief.*

Weiss, H. (2005). The afterschool evaluation symposium: Creating communities of practice to support quality afterschool programming. *Harvard Family Research Project, 1-18.* Washington, DC: C. S. Mott Foundation.

Williams, H. (2007, November). *Results: Duke–Durham neighborhood partnership.* Preliminary report prepared by the Rensselaerville Institute for The Duke Endowment.

Williams, H. (2008, March). *Duke–Durham neighborhood partnership: Results from the first decade.* Report prepared by the Rensselaerville Institute for The Duke Endowment.

York, P. (2003, June). Learning as we go: Making evaluation work for everyone. *The Conservation Company Briefing Paper, 1–11.*

Index

About the Author

Barbara C. Jentleson is currently an Assistant Professor of the Practice in the Program in Education at Duke University. From 2002 to 2010, she was the Director of Project HOPE, where she worked on the development of six community-based afterschool programs targeting low-income minority youth in Durham, North Carolina. Dr. Jentleson was the former principal of the Pathways School–Hyattsville, an alternative middle school for students with behavior and learning disabilities located in the Washington DC area. She has maintained a lifelong professional interest in developing learning environments that support the academic and social development of vulnerable children and youth.